The

Personal Journal

of

An Ordinary Person

Katharine Taylor Brennan, "An Ordinary Person:" 1943-1985

Katharine Taylor Brennan was born in Kingston, Ontario, and grew up in Brockville. She attended public school and high school in Brockville, earning prizes in mathematics and home economics. She also enjoyed success at public speaking, taking top honours in a Rotary Club-sponsored competition and representing Brockville at an experiment on Canadian citizenship sponsored by the Rotary Club.

Her final year of high school was spent at Neûchatel Junior College in Switzerland; she was active on the school magazine, and graduated with honours. She returned to Canada to attend Queen's University, earning her BA in 1965. After an extensive tour of Canada, the United States and Europe, she took a job at the YWCA in Brantford. Following another tour of Europe, she settled down as manager of book stores in Vancouver and then in Montreal.

Katharine was married in 1976 to Richard Brennan; they lived in Montreal after their marriage.

She loved the outdoors, especially swimming, camping, boating, cycling, bird-watching and gardening. As well as literature and her own writing, she enjoyed art and music and was a talented photographer.

Katharine gave her journal, along with permission to publish it, to her cousin Elizabeth Parsons Kirchner, who lovingly preserved it and, respecting a relative's wishes, delayed publication for some years after Katharine's death.

The Brennans kept in touch with a wide circle of friends and relatives of all ages, and Katharine credits her "network" with helping her during her illness. There is no doubt that any help they gave was amply rewarded: Katharine is the friend we all wish we had. Those of us who know her only through this journal also mourn her loss.

The
Personal Journal
of
An Ordinary Person

*I am such an ordinary person, and yet I lead such
an uncommon life. I love and am loved;
already that raises me above the usual sphere ...*

KATHARINE TAYLOR BRENNAN

Simon & Pierre
Toronto, Canada

Editor: Jean Paton
Design: Andy Tong
Illustrations: cover and pages 40, 64, 109 by K.T. Brennan

Printed and bound in Canada by Metrolitho.

The publication of this book was made possible by support from several sources. We would
like to acknowledge the generous assistance and ongoing support of **The Canada Council,
The Book Publishing Industry Development Program** of the **Department of Canadian
Heritage,** and **The Ontario Arts Council.**

J. Kirk Howard, President

1 2 3 4 5 • 0 9 8 7 6

Canadian Cataloguing in Publication Data
Brennan, Katharine Taylor, 1943-1985
    The personal journal of an ordinary person

ISBN 0-88924-265-8

1. Brennan, Katharine Taylor, 1943-1985.
2. Diabetics - Quebec (Province) - Biography.
3. Diabetics - Ontario - Biography. I. Title.

RC660.B74 1995   362.1'96462'0092   C95-930799-0

Order from Simon & Pierre Publishing Co. Ltd., c/o

Dundurn Press Limited	**Dundurn Distribution**	**Dundurn Press Limited**
2181 Queen Street East	73 Lime Walk	1823 Maryland Avenue
Suite 301	Headington, Oxford	P.O. Box 1000
Toronto, Canada	England	Niagara Falls, N.Y.
M4E 1E5	0X3 7AD	U.S.A. 14302-1000

The most important dates in my life:
April 16, 1943   my birth
August 16, 1944   Richard's birth
July 24, 1976   our marriage
June 2, 1934   my parent's marriage
December 3, 1905   my mother's birth
May 17, 1905   my father's birth

... and a few others – today, perhaps, or tomorrow.

July 12, 1979

The street is quiet, the summer heat is gone, the breeze follows the tune of a soft guitar. The night is mellow. Richard's voice is raw and rich with careful passion.

August 6

The first cool evening for many weeks. It has been a sniffy day with the tears finding a tiny crevice to follow over a too-smooth cheek.

The full moon, white and still, between two worn buildings. I destroy myself with wine and cigarettes. I walk a fine line, wavering between denial and indulgence. My laughter ripples the surface as my lungs dissolve and my bowels tremble. Where is the reality in dissolution? Where is the truth in denial? Where is the silence in excess?

Shall I just wait patiently for some answer from a friendly bystander? We slump in our places on some stray bus.

And what of the chance encounter on some street corner? "You like to remain anonymous," he says; the words echo through darkened alleys on my way home.

I am on my way; I am full of the smoke of a thousand lanterns.

It's a bit embarrassing to have been concerned with the human problem all one's life and find at the end that one has no more to offer by way of advice than "try to be a little kinder."
(Aldous Huxley)

August 7

What delicate lives we lead, what dangerous stakes we court in our perilous flight, what stupidities we encounter, what terrors we suffer at the folly we seek. And yet, what else is there? The safety of the harbour belies the lure of the open sea. One needs to be a gambler, one needs to know that he plays to lose, and that it is the sharp edge of the razor that finds its way to the bone, that draws forth a single drop of blood, that transforms an ordinary life into an elegant celebration.

They come to me, these women with all their uncertainties and fears and insecurities and hope, and look me straight in the eye, asking for this book or that, as if they were seeking to know the mystery of the universe. They beseech with their tired eyes; they have been trained to fulfill the needs of others and know not how to fulfill their own. And what of that? Shall we remain forever the mothers, the lovers, the caretakers, with our children, our men, our parents, our small household tasks, as we wash the dusty streets with our pails of clean water?

I have seen the tiny plants in the window, with too little sun; the laundry hung out in the rain; the empty cage hanging on the wire. And I have made a castle of sand on a stony beach and watched a child discover the pleasure of sand slipping through tiny fingers. I have seen a successful man weep at the sound of his own voice recalling the poems of his youth. I have seen the hesitant touch of young lovers, proper in the company of their elders, eager for solitude. I have seen delicate flowers growing out of the rock by the lake and through cracks in the pavement. I have seen the furious storm, the white-capped waves, the solid birch and the desperate pines bending to the will of the wind, and a sailboat that rode over the sudden sea to a safe harbour. And I have heard the crystal laughter of two women, strong and true, the presence of peace and goodwill, the silent source of deep comfort.

It is impossible to control creation. I don't mean this only in the sense of giving birth to new physical life. That which really is continues with the impetus which propelled its origin. I am and I am going on and on to the end of myself where something else begins.
(Evelyn Scott, from *Revelations: Diaries of Women*)

August 9

I cannot even imagine the experience of giving birth. I feel that I will remain ever unfulfilled as a woman until I experience the pain and the luxury of childbirth, the privilege that only a woman knows. How many times have I lived through this experience in my heart and mind, how many nights have I lain awake in anticipation and sorrow, feeling the emptiness of my womb. Is there not enough love in my being, not enough love in my loins, that I should be unable to conceive, to bear the joy and the burden of life within my body? I cannot satisfy this longing in any other way and I fear that my time is too short, that I cannot go further in my own growth without this. I am selfish and vain and impatient – and I wait with a heavy heart.

August 13

We wander through the maze of the book publishing industry, fascinated by the way each "rep" does his number. I like the old pros, who lay out their wares and let the books sell themselves.

August 16

They argue about love and death and sacrifice and the Holy Ghost, these three young men by the pay phone, standing on a concrete floor amidst the neon signs, the pinball machines and a screeching parrot. Over the relentless whir of cash registers, I hear the tall one beseech, "But He loves you. You have only to place your trust in Him. He will guide you in making the right decision."

It is so strange, this life, that everything takes place in an instant, that life and death, and peace and confusion co-exist. One man dies, another is born, another buys a map to guide him through the Metro system, a woman looks for spiritual sustenance in Hermann Hesse and Marquez and I bring her Lyall Watson's *Gift of Unknown Things*. She smiles; now able to finish reading Hesse and knowing that there are more discoveries to make, the fear of emptiness dissolves for awhile.

A man shoots his wife, then himself; she lives, he dies. A young boy disturbs the order of a grown-up's world and leaves, saying he will not return until Christmas. (We expect to see him tomorrow.) I bring a plant to hang in the store. The mystery of the universe remains intact.

And I sit in gratitude that both my father and I have lived long enough to have come through the fire and to have reached some understanding of and respect for each other.

Today is Richard's 34th birthday.

August 17

Midnight, sometime after. I am restless, I eat a few carrots from the stew pot and polish off a handful of unsalted almonds. Have been watching my sodium intake for three weeks and have eliminated certain physical annoyances by doing so – swelling ankles, sore legs, retention of water. Wonder if my blood pressure is down, too – expect that it is. So much for the mundane.

Start to feel that I have a certain control over my life. I am better able to express and fulfill my needs – more aware of the needs of others and have a deep sense of caring about those who are close to me.

I puzzle over the literature of women and this rampant discontent that surfaces, the burdens that will not be laid down, the heaviness that we drag behind us or hold unsteadily in our arms. I see myself and others totter along the sidewalks clutching our groceries and our children, trying to maneuver throughout crowds and turnstiles, grateful when someone else opens the door for us.

To be a woman is to be a juggler, to weigh this need against another, to shift the burden, toss it up in the air for a moment and center oneself so that one may catch it again more gracefully.

August 18

Listening to my mother's voice – a conversation that I taped in Brockville about Annie Laurie and Aunt Annie – making a copy of it for Betty. A treasure that I cannot fathom. To think that years hence when my mother is gone, when I am gone, her exuberant laughter and raucous voice will remain. They say that sound echoes through the universe forever. Are we surrounded by waves, by voices that we do not hear?

August 22

"Time is a jet plane; it moves too fast" (a line from a song that I only slightly recall). Sometimes I am too busy, too occupied by the immediacy of events to record their passing, too much at the control of an external life, at the mercy of outward demands that command my attention. I feel the pull, the tension, and I thrive on it. I drown myself in the energy available. I am the dancer and the dance – spinning carelessly through empty space.

I watch children at play on a great revolving wheel. They grasp the circular bar, run to make it spin faster, and swing freely when their growing legs can no longer reach the ground. Faster and faster they fly through the air. Sometimes one falls and another takes his place. They wait eagerly for the chance to grab hold – and when they fall, it is always with laughter. I marvel that they never seem to hurt themselves. They seem to know when the moment is right. They live in the moment and understand its vicissitudes.

> *The newspaper lies, the radio lies, the TV lies;*
> *the streets howl with the truth.*
>
> (Henry Miller)

August 23

I see the things that blind me. I see the traps I set for myself. I see how easy it is to become ensnared in my own designs, ambitions, fears, possessions. I see that I do not want freedom. And that I desire it above all else.

I see that it is desire itself that constricts and creates bonds and barriers. I see that I am schizoid and I see that the struggle between yes and no is the most powerful force in the universe.

I am a woman and I rejoice. I am silence, and I say too much. A line from Einstein – misquoted as usual, as I only vaguely remember it – that imagination is more important than knowledge. I think he means that spark, that instant of discovery that we all cherish, that we all lust after, the magic moment, "the timeless moment in the rose garden" of T. S. Eliot. (THAT is not a misquote; it is one that I have remembered intact from the midnight readings of my youth.)

I look at myself in the mirror of some dime store window as I pass by on a street full of strangers, and I catch a glimpse of a worn-out body that walks proud and resolute through a maze, a labyrinth of conflicting emotions and bittersweet thoughts.

I write from the inside of myself and save the spoken word for acquaintances. I want to fill these fine white pages with my random scrawl, like a sometimes desperate note scribbled on the last scrap of paper, carefully stuffed into a bottle found on the beach and cast hopefully, and with deliberate abandon, into the sea. There is such trust in me that I believe in my own worth, in the value of mankind, in the soul of humanity.

No, I do not save all my small thoughts, my tender emotions for these pages – I give them freely, at times, to whomever comes by. Sometimes it is just a smile for the beggar on the corner or a casual remark to the grocer. Love could be so simple.

I seek life in all the old familiar places and spaces, of which there are many, and in which there is (occasionally) much openness and much curiosity towards the mysteries of life and its infinite variety, its myriad forms. It is an inexplicable wonder and remains forever mysterious and elusive.

All of life is necessary; one form cannot exist without the other; each conflicts and complements, struggles for existence and proclaims its right to life, its search for the source, which is itself the alpha and omega, the mystic spiral that eternally recreates itself. Although a particular form may pass beyond itself and be transformed into another realm of being, it will never cease to be somewhere, everywhere, anywhere.

Even when (and if) we know who we are and where we are going, the mystery will remain; we can never solve the riddle. We are part of the riddle, we are a part of the universe of uncertainty, we are temporary and universal at the same time. We exist outside of time and space and other man-made illusions. Whatever our coordinates, whatever our boundaries, whatever prisons we have created for ourselves, whatever rules we have constructed to allow ourselves to perpetuate that myth of bondage, we cannot escape the process, cannot escape the cycle from which we arise and to which we will inevitably return in the final moment, which is only just another moment that contains within itself the infinite multitude of all moments that have ever existed and which will continue to be born anew in each glimmer of life.

We watch a baseball game on TV, Richard and Bill and David and I. There are thousands of people there singing together the national anthem, and somehow it doesn't matter – all nationalities, races, creeds dissolve. It is just men and women joined together for a moment, some silent, some singing heartily. We are all the same, excessively human; simple beings joined for an instant in common song.

I have never been able to sing "O Canada," or any hymn, with a group of my fellow beings without tears. The day that I am able to sing a hymn straight through will be the day I have lost my humanity.

August 23

Today I could care less about anyone – the damned jostling crowds, short-tempered people, screaming children, crooked old men, jeweled and powdered women weighed down by their trinkets and their lives, the doughnut-munching mob that descends on a raining Saturday afternoon, the Alexis Nihon Plaza, a zoo full of strong creatures that wear human bodies and consume the printed page like vultures at a picnic. I want to lie in my warm bed all day and listen to rain on the roof.

12

Is it always thus – that I love and hate in the same breath? The capacity for both is ever present.

I wander down the Boulevard of Broken Dreams (our pet name for St. Lawrence Boulevard). They have blocked off the street from Sherbrooke to Duluth for a four-day festival, and through the revelling mass I catch a glimpse of a troupe of young Portuguese dancers performing the tarantella. All exhaustion evaporates and I return home refreshed.

August 24

If only I had enough time! It is clear to me, after much torment and useless suffering, that time is exactly what I don't have, that time is beyond my control. So it becomes a very rational decision that is against my nature, against my emotional indulgence.

I strive for a kind of perfection that perhaps is unreasonable. I wanted to find the magic, to make it work, forgetting that one can never make magic work, that magic is a gift, that it comes unbidden and does not respond to one's will, one's selfishness. Yes, it requires effort, but I get lost in the effort and reach to find a balance, need to know when to suspend the effort and let magic have its way. To strive, to search – but to remain open to the gift of magic, to receive what is offered always as a precious gem.

Our desires, our striving, our needs so often get in the way of what is constantly being offered freely. We are not open to what is free – we are too busy trying to find freedom.

No fear, no hate, no pain, no broken heart.
(Eurythmics)

August 27

We are all prisoners of freedom.

Well, I suppose that statement deserves some elucidation. First of all, I love these lines that appear out of nowhere, that come unbidden on street corners while waiting for the green light or when I am sitting in the laundromat watching the spin-dry cycle. Sometimes I relish the words like an aphrodisiac. And who could bear to discover their meaning? There is more to words than mere meaning, and it is fine just to speak, to hear, to let the words drift and play, to savour the sound and delight in being able to express simple thoughts or complex ones without having to discern their significance.

Yes, what does it mean, this phrase, we are all prisoners of freedom? Can we ever understand what it meant at the moment of writing? In my very attempt to fathom its undertones, its nuances, I become enmeshed, caught in a web of cerebral association that is the antithesis of freedom and leaves me far from any real understanding.

Ah, yes, now I know what I wish to say – and I relate one of yesterday's experiences. We spent some time with Paul and Rick who brought with them a friend who is a concert pianist. We talked a while and I wanted very much to cut the chatter and play a piece of recorded music while he was here, a piano composition of Beethoven (the *Pathetique Sonata*) – yes, I admit, to see what he would do, to enter his space as it were, to find out where he lives. And I wanted to see the reaction of Richard, who, being steeped in the folk and country tradition, mildly disdains classical music, having had only slight exposure to it.

We listened. The room fell silent, Paul and Rick slumped in their chairs ... I curious, Richard uneasy, and Claude alert. And then Claude started to do this marvelous thing; he began to give us his understanding of the *emotional* quality of the music – an interpretation, so to speak, with a few words here and there, a refined gesture, a wave of his hand, a sigh, a subtle posture. Richard put aside his previous prejudices and the light burned in his eyes. Claude opened up a space for all of us to hear the incredible spectrum of emotional subtlety in the music. And I realized, later, that it was not so much the actual words that Claude spoke that gave me an insight into the piece of music, but the *way* in which he spoke them; even more important, the way in which he, Claude, listened to the music, and his love for it, and his desire for us all to enter that invisible and arcane universe.

He has invited us to come to his humble lodgings to listen to him play on his grand piano. I feel so blessed sometimes.

August 30

The days are so full I feel like I live through several lifetimes in twenty-four hours. I am the housekeeper, I work in the bookstore, I meet with my financial advisor, I apologize to a young girl for a gaffe, I talk cinema with a stranger from Greece, I listen to Franck's *Symphony,* I go back to work, and later I will wash the kitchen floor. One would not say that I lead a dull life. I could not live without variety. I have never been content doing one thing at a time.

It strikes me that one of the main problems in communication is that we all have diverse ways of doing the same task and that much misunderstanding often results from this. How often have I heard, "Hey, that's not the way to do that," and how often I've thought, "But that's not the way *I* do it." And I see how stuck I am in my own little way of doing something although *my* way is not necessarily the best way but only an habitual mechanism to which I slavishly adhere and defend at all costs.

How easy it would be to learn a new way. It costs so little to consider another way, to consider another person's reality, and perhaps learn a valuable lesson – to admit, yes, that this person is really good at this or that, and learn from them. It seems so ridiculous that we are all so identified with our ways and our attitudes and our habits, that to give up even one of them seems like a denial of self, a threat to our sense of self-determination. What is so precious about *my* way that I could not dare to try another? Is my way through life bound by such trivialities?

August 31

A pleasant-faced old sage rests on the church steps, mottled in the sunshine like a Monet painting with his white-brimmed straw hat and beige loafers. An old woman, face in the shadow under her black scarf, shoulders hunched to the task, makes her way through the hurried mass. A black woman stands in the shadow of an old building holding her copy of *Awake!* in front of her like a shield; a young woman, confused and angry, she can find no one who speaks her language. A broad man with a broad grin and a broad Stetson hat speaks flawless French and the King's English, puts his arm around his friend and says, "We're both ex-Indian Army – that was the time when men were men and women were women." A middle-aged lady in a sterile high-rise office babbles nervously at me to relieve her loneliness and isolation. Sights and sounds of another day.

I reflect on an old saying of Charlotte Whitton [mayor of Ottawa 1951-1956, 1961-1964] that a woman has to do things twice as well as a man to be thought half as good, or, like Ginger Rogers, has to do everything backwards and in high heels to keep in step. I try not to believe that, but my experience tells me that it is too true. I feel the pressure almost crushing me at times.

Today I am clinging desperately to a flimsy tree whose tenuous roots are barely attached to a barren rock overlooking an abyss. At times I feel that to fall headlong into the abyss is preferable to clinging to the rock. I am not sure that I want to struggle with the forces of gravity.

You really find out what gravity is when you try to pull yourself up.
(Richard, on doing chin-ups)

September 7

Life feels, at times, like one long drawn-out commercial, and I'm not sure what is being advertised or if I am supposed to buy or sell.

Lost souls who wander through the labyrinth with no direction home, whose attention is riveted by jukeboxes and stoplights and glossy-covered publications: where do we all get off?

September 15

This morning on the way to work I see the bewildered eyes of a ten-year-old child as he watches his father being carried out of the funeral parlor in a large brown box. And tonight on the way home I pass a string of honking long black sedans carrying newlyweds. These vehicles that mark our transitions.

You haunted her grave with your flowers ...
(Unknown)

September 17

My silent kitchen, early evening, 9 p.m. The dishes are half-washed, I have picked off the dead leaves from the plants that grow in profusion in every window. I have a sore throat and have need to ward off an incipient malady with a dish of hot peppers and zucchini and a tumbler full of iced Southern Comfort. My chest is heavy with fiery breath. The autumn vapors are upon us.

We share our tourtière and home-baked apple pie with Bill, Richard's friend of many lifetimes, a poet of the streets who wanders through the alleyways, welcoming the shadows and the sun's rays alike. Women pass and are blessed with his glance. Sunshine and pigeons pecking the resistant pavement for a few crumbs. An acrobat slides down a thin wire on his head for a few dollars and a moment of adulation from the crowd.

Yesterday a woman gingerly plucks a book from a precarious pile of assorted volumes. *A Season in Hell* it is called, and she says to me, "That's what I am going through; a season in Hell. Well, not me, really, but my friend. He is ill, a successful man. He had to give it all up, his work, his success, his ambition. And I must watch him. It is hard to see a grown man die."

We talk, standing there amidst the glaring lights and the blaring disco sounds of a Saturday plaza dance contest. She looks at my awkward yet sympathetic eyes and says, like some kind of ethereal messenger, "At thirty-five, you think you know it all, and at sixty, you know that there is still much to learn." And she says, "I probably sound like an old fool."

And I say, "To me, you sound very wise."

She smiles and pays $2.95. "I try to be," she utters as the music blares "Get Up and Boogie."

A rumpled "rubby," a master of the panhandle trade, stumbles into my antiseptic, dust-free universe and demands, "I need twenty-five cents for the bus." He peers at me through ancient, hollow eyes as I fumble in my macramé white bag for a bus ticket. I know what he wants, and in my perversity I want to meet and somehow defeat his artful dodgery, to let him know that I am wise to his deception. I produce a crisp green ticket and he says to me with great aplomb, "You don't understand." And, with some conceit and a slight measure of disdain, tempered by infinite compassion and humble complicity, I hand him a quarter. Who can refuse a man his life? Who am I to judge the life of another?

And then there is Mary, with whom I have worked for three days – a terrified woman of some forty-odd years, with her lacquered, manicured hair and her nervous hum, trying so desperately to become part of our hermetic world. I am aware that I shut her out, that I guard my silly secrets well, that I pleasantly, but blatantly, exhibit my talents and my efficiency, that I make her feel deficient. I parade around the store, doing this and that, secure in my element, ego-strong, showing her what's what: that I'm not just Richard's wife, that I know what the book business is all about.

The power of youth and energy! Strutting my stuff like a precocious peacock. Some part of me does not want her to be here. I want her to know that she does not fit. I listen to her tell her life story, I encourage her to speak, and yet I do not want to be a part of her life, her troubled cracked smile that speaks of compromise and defeat. A husband who left her and married her best friend, her children who preferred to live with "the other family" – a woman who walks along the lake shore late at night and claims that she is not afraid and lonely. I do not want to be drawn into her misery, her vacuum. There is something silent, some deep tragedy that I do not want to be a part of.

And yet I am curious. I want to understand, but only on my own terms. I think about love, about loving other people, and I see, but only slightly, that it is easy to love someone on my own terms, and oh so difficult to love them on theirs. There is so much that I dislike about the mass of humanity, always the want, the demand that disturbs me, the *need* that I can never fill. Why is it that we gravitate, even demand from others that *they* should fulfill *our* lives? Why do we *demand* so much from life itself, when in fact it is life itself that has given us the very source of our being? We all have burdens to bear; we could laugh and cry together. Is it too much to ask?

Tomorrow I must work again, must dust the shelves and count the change, straighten the books and be pleasant to customers. Tonight I relish the silence at my window.

October 5

A few days have passed, days full of anger and sickness. Today for the first time in many days I feel "normal." I mean that I am capable of coping with my reactions without too much trauma.

October 14

Strange how a series of events can bring me back to myself. Strange that the efforts we make, the desires, the unspoken wishes are answered, the emptiness is filled; how easily the confusion is banished.

Last weekend, Thanksgiving with Richard, both Moms and Dads, Ted and Debbie. I spend the two days at the cottage building the fire, gathering twigs and dry wood to keep the place warm, tending the precarious flame, up early in the grey, windy dawn to make sure that there is a welcome fire for the rest. A fine turkey feast of renewal and warmth amidst my family. A quiet conversation with Debbie over white wine and nostalgic reflection. My father says to me in his stern but loving fashion, "Nature in the raw is seldom mild." For a moment, we are all raw, children of nature, and we all take part in this annual celebration, for a moment thankful that we share our lives together. And through the drudgeful days of dusty shelves, dirty sheets and desolate streets come old friends who bring their lives to exchange experiences around our long red table – Harriet, Rob, George.

I am not writing well tonight; the words do not say what I feel.

October 21

I need to find ways to effectively express tensions and unfulfilled needs. How easy it is to dump the responsibility on someone else and let them take the blame for what I am unable to do for myself. I seem to be so full of inexpressible needs these days, and I withdraw when I can find no effective way to fill myself, only to have those needs surface again with a vengeance. And then the pressure becomes too much to deal with and I explode in a rage and am always guilty afterwards. Senseless cycle. I want this, I want that, I want something else, ever restless, ever unsatisfied, ever discontent, no end to it except in rare moments of simplicity.

October 26

There is something about the way we reveal ourselves in everything we do, the way we are what we are in every moment, yet life unfolds as it is with no interference from our little designs.

I love to be in the presence of men when they are just as they are; Richard and Bill sitting with their guitars and their dreams of poetry and music, my father dictating a letter while I type it for him, strong in his element, intense, centered, involved in his task, dressed in his habitual pajamas, a cigarette dangling, glass in hand.

November 5

A weekend in Kingston, Richard and I helping his parents prepare for winter like a family of squirrels. We raked leaves, spread Winter-Kill over the lawn, gathered kindling and split wood. I felt so content. Returned here to find that another creature, a mouse, had raided the garbage bag in the back to feather her nest. We all have the same thing in mind.

December 8

I am such an ordinary person and yet I lead such an uncommon life. I love and am loved; already that raises me above the usual sphere. It seems to me important that I do each task with a certain sense of responsibility, both of credit and blame. For each action that I instigate, there is a recognition that it is I who does it – and that I draw inspiration from another source. I do not wish to know from whence it comes – only that it *is*.

I feel that it is important to take the time to do something special for those I love – for those I have chosen to be bound to – and for those who have chosen me.

I am capable of being consumed by the flame, like seasoned wood that burns more brightly for those who know how to feed the fire. Sometimes I am like green branches that will not burn without much effort. Sometimes I ignite and burn uncontrollably like a blazing holocaust. But mostly I seek the hand that will judiciously kindle the tender outpourings of my soul and nurture the flame as it flickers and despairs of going out in its prime.

It is time to put my life on the line, on the razor's edge.
(K.T.B.)

March 21, 1980

Halifax, Nova Scotia. Flying. I always have this overwhelming urge to cry as the plane makes its descent to earth. Falling through a screen of clouds; falling, falling, like the plunge of a reluctant diver to the bottom of the sea. For a moment, I float above it all, and too soon the solid earth rises to greet me and enfold me in its vast embrace.

From the silence of flight to coffee cups and wooden tables. The sun radiates from somewhere above. A window cleaner washes away the dusty rain drops, whistling as he works. A sad woman in a brown felt hat nibbles her dry toast. It is 11:30 a.m. Friday. I want to take her picture. She catches my eye as I raise the camera, and I lower it. Not here, she says, not here.

Wolfville, Nova Scotia. Walked out to where the sidewalk ends and drifted away with the smoke. Joni Mitchell sweetens the late afternoon's passage. I am a passenger who pauses along the way to listen to the other voices, other longings, other echoes. Today I ride on the wind, lightly touch the ground and reach for the sky. I climb a mountain where many paths cross and converge. I feel the chill of winter evaporate and return again. I smell the leaves of autumn covered with ice and I hear a train rushing past in the distance.

March 24 and 25

St. John's, Newfoundland. The landscape rushes by outside the bus window. Our flight to St. John's is rerouted to Gander and I get a bonus five-hour bus ride to St. John's through the countryside – snow-covered, fog, ancient pines, barren fields, rocky shore curving alongside Trinity Bay. The wind howls and buffets our journey. I see rain and I am content to be a part of this rugged land, these hardy people who are close to the movements of nature and the turbulent sea. I am content to wander through crooked streets and steep inclines, but I am a stranger here and I know it – a dog chases me out of his territory, another cowers and hides behind a tree; an old man stares out to sea and only gives me a passing glance, another says, "Good day." A sailor whistles as I scour the docks for weather-beaten faces and traces of Celtic voices. The insistent wind carries me through rain and sleet to the top of Signal Hill where the mournful foghorn rises to enchant and free my spirit. A lone bird calls out my name and I reach for its wing. I do not want to wager with the storm too long and I retreat to the warmth of home-made soup and hot coffee.

March 26

St. John's, Newfoundland. The sun came out and my nostalgia and sadness of the past two days evaporated. Checked out the museum where a white-haired gentleman showed me old photographs of Newfoundland from the early 1900's. Took a cab up Signal Hill. (I got halfway yesterday but the wind and rain drove me down to the valley.) Magnificent view, but again the wind overwhelmed me and I hiked back down the long, winding road. I meet few pilgrims on the way up.

Martha's Bar last night, where I recorded a local singer-guitarist reminiscent of voices from the past. Now I sit in Shelley's Restaurant and hear sounds from the present. A black horse stands on a grassy slope facing the wind; a stream of pale blue water is at his feet, the sky radiates azure reflections. Will he cross over to the fields beyond? I am unsure that there is any future here, chained to the rocks and the unforgiving wind, the unpredictable sea.

I have the privilege of no longer being young.
(K.T.B.)

March 28

St. John, New Brunswick. Stayed up all night to catch a 5 a.m. ferry from Digby, Nova Scotia, to here – a very old city that is trying hard to catch up to modern times. At the busiest intersection in the city there is no traffic light, yet the system works – these maritimers are a strange lot. An indoor market with some interesting faces in the crowd.

April 6

Brockville train station. These phantom black beasts that storm out of the dark night, roaring and spitting fire, belching steam and shrieking metal against metal as I stand on an empty platform waiting to be engulfed by its raw power. Exhausted and sultry am I as I wrap myself in solitude and drift quietly through the spaces in my world.

April 18

A few days after it has happened, I write of a remarkable experience. The morning that I left for work with my world falling apart, breaking, splitting, wrenching, searing, losing balance – a feeling of having lost everything, a feeling of profound failure torments me. My father who is ill, my husband with whom I can only rarely communicate, a script that I cannot write, eyes that will not see clearly, a heel that falls off my shoe as I stalk the pavement. I get on the bus. It is crowded. The driver takes off in a hell of a hurry. I lose my balance and waver unsteadily, about to crash through the front window with my too-heavy bag and a parcel of books. No chance to find equilibrium. And out of nowhere a black man reaches out his hand to steady me and prevents my fall.

Tonight I clean out drawers and divest myself of paper burdens. The *I Ching* says temporary obstruction.

Odette and Paul present me with a Korean parasol to keep off the rain showers. I hang it high in the dining room and watch the blue light cast its spell. Gram Parsons sings about brass buttons, green silk and silver shoes. It is spring outside, hearts on fire.

Betty sends a birthday card of grace, balance, beauty; she says it is me. I wonder. Richard says I look nice tonight. I say, "What do you mean?" So uncertain, so defensive and LOCKED IN.

I am thirty-seven.

I buy a large orange pot to make soup in. I go back to the wine and oblivion. I think about the pencils I will sharpen tomorrow, I do the income tax, I wash dishes, I look at old material bought in a moment's flight of fancy. I see the dried flowers gathered last fall, the greying photos on the wall, the lists of things to do to keep the hounds from the door.

I trip over cracks in the pavement. I wash my hair, I dream, I read my mother's notes about a trip to Newfoundland in 1938 and a poem by Heinrich Heine about two lovers who have so carefully concealed themselves from each other in a game of hide-and-seek that they are in danger of never finding each other again.

If you want tomorrow to be different, you must make today different.
(George Gurdjieff)

May 23

Sudden change. My eyes have been quite stable for over a year – until yesterday at 2 p.m. Like a slap in the face, my bad eye (thank God it's the bad one) clouds over and reduces my already useless vision to nothing but light and shadow. My field of sight narrows and I try not to withdraw into that hazy world. Fortunately, I have a great store of anger which has saved me more than once from acute depression. At least rage is a form of communication, and I use it to keep the fire alive. The danger is always not to be consumed by it. Again I am at my best when I have to struggle with something. It is hell for those around me.

I wonder what direction my life will take from here.

July 3

Hardly thought that I'd be making this entry in this book, the handbag Richard gave me and all its contents having been stolen two days before our trip to California. I bought another journal for the trip and said silent goodbyes to these pages. There was some part of me, though, that knew that these emblazoned lines would find their way back to me – and they did, via a remarkably honest taxi driver and a chain of events that still mystifies me. Well, there is still some mystery left. Let it be.

We have a dinner party with Paul and Rick and Martha and Bob and we talk around a candle flickering in the backyard, surrounded by green plants, a child playing on the balcony next door and a cool breeze calming the darkness.

What do I want to say? Something that keeps ringing in my head – Richard's cousin said it. You can spend ten years getting ready to walk out on that stage, but what happens when someone boos you when you've spent all that time getting to the point where you think you're the best you can be? Instead, he said, you should be out on that stage now, while you're still learning, so if they boo you, it's not all that important anyway. But what a crusher to spend all that energy only to find out that you've been in the dark so long that the stage lights blind you.

July 10

Baumgardt Island, St. Lawrence River: My ancestral home, to which I return for peace and rejuvenation. We have been here for about a week, Richard and I. The daily events are recorded in the camp diary – but tonight, what I have to say is too personal for general reading. My eyes have become worse – my good eye is hemorrhaging badly and I can barely see what I am writing or read what I have written. It seems that the time now is short before I will be forced to invent a new lifestyle.

This frail world is such an anxious place, full of unnameable shadows and unseen obstacles. These days, every time I do something there is always a moment's pause when I wonder how much longer I will be able to do this.

Because I have difficulty seeing things close at hand, it forces me to concentrate on what I am doing – no more automatic reflexes. My movements are much more deliberate. I can still drive the car, as distance vision is okay. I need to be busy, to keep trying to do things. What I fear most is becoming dependent on others, losing my sense of freedom and being unable to survive by my own resources and capabilities. It frightens me to know that I will be so vulnerable and it disturbs me that I may become bitter and closed. I wonder how strong are my instincts for survival.

I bought a red pen to see if I can read any more clearly with it. Well, it seems to be okay – but I'm having trouble seeing the side of the page. I can manage if I'm careful. What a lot of energy all this is taking. Everything I do is a challenge.

It takes all my energy just to get through the day. It takes me twice, if not three times, as long to do anything, and I have to double-check to make sure I have not forgotten anything, have not left some essential lying behind, like my house key, wallet, etc. My spirits are starting to lag as I think of the impossibilities ahead.

I went to work for a few hours today and suffered silently as customers sighed impatiently when I asked them to tell me the price of the books. I suppose I'll get over that. I will become a more compassionate person, that's for sure, at least after I get through all the bitterness and anger at allowing other people's unconscious reactions to make me feel so stupid and helpless.

Yesterday I burned my arm, today I dropped my hat in the mud, forgot my tobacco in the store, burned the beans, and someone picked up my bag of olives before I had a chance to notice what had happened – hassles all day, ordinary events that under the circumstances take on exaggerated proportions and reinforce this vulnerability that I have acquired in the last few days.

It is always such little incidents that break us. Major crises are somehow easier to deal with. It's all these annoying details. I trip over cracks in the pavement, but somehow manage to avoid the wide crevasses.

Five Dozen Bran Muffins
(Pat Sabourin)

5 1/2 c. flour	1 qt. buttermilk or sour milk
2 1/2 c. sugar	1 1/2 c. cooking oil
3 c. bran	4 eggs
2 c. all bran	1/2 c. molasses
3 Tbsp. baking soda	2 c. raisins

1. Combine first 4 ingredients.
2. Stir soda and buttermilk.
3. Add oil, eggs and molasses; beat well.
4. Pour liquid into dry ingredients.
5. Add raisins.
6. Grease muffin tins and bake at 375^0 for 20-25 minutes.

July 16

Tonight I was standing on St. Lawrence Boulevard, waiting to cross the street after my swim, and some lady backed into me with her car. Scared the hell out of me.

I don't seem to be able to do much else in the evening except write in this book – can't sew or read or type letters. I've run out of floors to wash, cupboards to clean, people to talk to on the phone.

Will have to learn how to play music again. Can't seem to get out of this preoccupation with my eyes. It is wearing me out. I am slowly trying to get my life together, and it is agonizing at times.

July 17

Sitting in the laundromat waiting for the spin-dry cycle to complete its business. Today I can almost see what I am writing. Managed to get through the morning at the store without once having to ask a customer the price on the book. Now I am as intolerant as ever of other people's infirmities. An old man blithely ambles to the head of the line at the bank and steps in front of me. I turn to the guy behind me and say in my most caustic tones, "Well, I guess that's how you get ahead in this world; step to the head of the line as if the rest of us don't exist." Then it dawns on me how intolerant I am with my youth and strength and ego. The minute I start to feel my own power returning, I start to knock down the failings of others. Such games we play with our lives.

Later, 10 p.m. After the thundering rain of early morning it is cool tonight. My beans in the backyard barely survived the pelting. They have all fallen over and are lying limply on the ground. The sun will revive them – that and a bit of string which I will use tomorrow to tie them up.

Sat down and spent two hours writing a resumé of my life for a job application. As Richard's mother said to me the other night in the depths of my depression and barely concealed terror, "Well, Kathy, you just have to go ahead and do what you're going to do as if everything will be all right." The wisest piece of common sense that anyone has ever given me.

So here I go again reaching for the brass ring. I still have certain difficult decisions to make, primarily about having children. I don't think or feel that I can afford to take the risk of blindness, kidney failure and possible damage to the child. I haven't yet mentioned anything to Richard, but it is on my mind constantly. After these last ten days of extremely limited sight I know now that I am not willing to sacrifice what precious little vision I have for a child. It is so hard to give up a dream. I keep vacillating, putting it off, wanting someone else to take the responsibility for that decision.

July 19

I read somewhere that you only become truly creative once you understand and accept your limitations. Yup – I'm beginning to know what that means. I think that all possibilities are open to me, but I'm too caught up in that dream to face reality and act on it. Acting of any kind is impossible in the dream world, in the realm of imagination. And all creativity by its very nature is active. What price must one pay for a few simple truths?

"All right," I said. "I'll do something different with my pork chops."
(Advertisement in *Woman's Day*)

July 21

Ted and Debbie for supper Saturday night. John and his girlfriend Debbie arrived for a few hours yesterday from Ottawa. Seems everyone has a friend named Debbie. Walked around Old Montreal, taking in the street life; clowns, sidewalk artists, musicians. Went into the sailors' church (Bon Secours) and Notre Dame Cathedral. Coffee and beer at Stash's. Made chili sauce, cherry jam, strawberry-orange jam and nectarine preserves.

Keeping busy; working three hours a day in Richard's store. Rain every day; my garden is drowning, but I am keeping my head above water. I have breakfast at my favourite restaurant – Irv's Place, a real greasy spoon that serves great scrambled eggs and toast with peanut butter. I record the mundane events of my days as I try to sort out the larger dramas that play with my spirit.

Bill Furey has published his first book of poems; our friend Bob Del Tredici is publishing his first book of interviews and photographs on Three Mile Island in October. The times are ripe for something.

Tonight I tossed my gum (green) in the salad, thinking it was a piece of green onion. Tastes great with oil and vinegar. My mistakes are becoming a great source of humour.

July 24

Our fourth anniversary. Strange dreams last night about Blue and Chickey. As always the sense of protection and unconditional trust is strong in my dog dreams – and now it seems entirely possible that one day I may again need a dog to get me through the streets. Somehow it doesn't frighten me, the possibility of being dependent on a dog. But being dependent on other people does. I am slowly learning to accept help from others when I need it, but it is difficult to make that admission.

I feel that I grew up on the wrong side of the tracks – I should have learned early to be a street fighter. But I was always told, oh, you'll never have to worry about anything – you have everything you need. I grew up protected and sheltered and naive. It is only now that I have begun to learn how to survive and that is taking every ounce of strength and resilience I have.

Jean said to me the other day, "When did you first feel vulnerable?" I answered: when I was about twelve. Later I realized that was about the time that Chickey was taken away to a farm in the country, partly because he was getting old but also because he had become unmanageable. Shortly thereafter I stopped eating for six months and lost fifty pounds. I think I could have accepted Chickey's death better than his untimely removal. I never did find out what happened to him. He was my closest friend as a child – he and my imaginary friends Debbie and Dakey. I don't remember what happened to them either. I think they are still climbing trees at the cottage. I hear them every now and then in the early morning when I am there.

Dinner at the Bal St. Louis. Richard gives me an ivory bird to hang on the gold chain around my neck and a teardrop-shaped box inlaid with mother-of-pearl.

July 31

Working in the Montreal indoor shopping mall "2020," a labyrinth of mirrors and lights and red escalators that carry stunned-looking shoppers through these sleazy catacombs. A strange crowd.

This afternoon I sit in the laundromat, hardly able to breathe in the heat, listening to the *Moonlight Sonata* on the radio and remembering conversations of the past few days.

A violent young man sits beside me on the train from Toronto and talks of tornadoes in the desert, of gathering jewels in Malaysia and of killing off all those in power. He talks of warriors and slaves and masters and sleepwalkers and his eyes dart over the passengers, searching out any possible threat or perhaps his next victim. He does not terrify me; he is not what he says he is. He is probably even more dangerous than he thinks he is, but he is even more asleep than the ones around him whom he mocks and despises. A strange young man.

And yesterday in the store a dashing Spaniard says, "The women, they should stay home and make the sex."

August 1

My demon doubt raises its little signpost and pickets my energy bank. I seem to be having a constant battle between over-confidence and total lack of it. The yes-I-can, no-I-can't syndrome. It is very tiring. My eyes are at least functioning to some degree, but my energy level vacillates wildly and unpredictably. I can't depend on my body to carry me through the day. I take cat naps on the bus but feel a general sense of exhaustion and depletion.

September 2

Labour Day weekend at the cottage. A couple of days of internal and external stress closely followed by absolute stillness. Human nature and great nature playing havoc with the elements.

September 14

Vision has been back to normal since the end of July. Tonight I go to see a healer from England. I am beginning to explore avenues of self-healing through foot reflexology, massage and breathing. I am only just beginning to understand the incredibly complex mechanism that is our body. It is miraculous that it works at all. I am anxious to learn as much as I can.

The landscape soothes me as it rushes by the bus window on my way to and from Ottawa to see Grandma Brennan. One might say that the road is infinitely boring. For me, it calms my rough edges and fills in the spaces. Even the slow drizzle is somehow satisfying and appropriate for reflection.

October 16

Have been ill for the last month. In hospital for almost two weeks – leg infection, bleeding stomach and apparently a miscarriage.

Sometimes being prepared is only false confidence.
(K.T.B.)

January 16, 1981

Today, I suppose, is as good a day as any to start writing again. A kind of chronicle, this is an account of the process that is my life.

I am feeling sorry for myself these days because I have almost lost my eyesight and am in the final stages of hanging on to an old way of life. Some changes will have to be made soon and I have not yet found the energy to make them. I would rather lie in my bed and dream about all the things I am going to do when I can see again. For the moment, I stubbornly continue doing the things I have always done, a little slower, perhaps, a little less meticulously.

An elderly gentleman came into the store the other day to look at the books. He browsed for a few minutes then walked over to the cash register with one of the recent best-sellers. "Could you tell me the price," he asked quietly. "A little trouble with the eyes," he added as he pulled out a small pocket magnifying glass.

Not to be outdone by this admission, I quickly retrieved my slightly larger magnifying glass from behind the cash register and with some difficulty read him the price.

"Oh, I see you have one of those too," he remarked. "Mine's quite strong, you know. Let's see yours." For the next few minutes we compared lenses like a couple of jewelers examining rough-cut diamonds. Finally the old gentleman leaned closer to me and declared in conspiratorial tones, "You know, they tell me I'm legally blind and shouldn't be walking about by myself. Want me to carry a white cane, they do, but that would make me feel too old. "Besides," he whispered, "I'm only eighty-four."

Yesterday I told Robert and Jean that I might not be able to continue working much longer because of my eyes. We talked at length and as we talked I found myself saying, yes I could probably manage to do such and such and yes, with a little help, I could still do that, etc. Strange, isn't it, that it seems almost more difficult for other people to admit that I can't see, that things will have to change. We ended the conversation by agreeing to leave things as they are, and everyone seemed much relieved – and we can pretend for the time being that everything is as it was before. It disturbed me a little, how easy it is to allow the comfortable familiarity of habit to drown out the desperate reality of my present situation. For now, I rely on habit and memory to get me through.

Dance to the tension of a world on the edge.
(St. Lawrence Blvd. graffiti)

January 31

Light. It flickers through the green plants hanging at my bedroom window and falls in bars on the floor. It is winter and I know that my plants are dying. There is not enough light, yet they stubbornly refuse to relinquish their tenuous grasp. Light. It slices like a knife through the water, carving its legacy into rock and tree, stone and brick and glass. It plummets through molecules, chiseling its passage through space – warming, drying, scorching, blinding. It is not gentle nor subtle in its blatant bid for supremacy.

Light. It charms the dark, casting a spell over the blackness, banishing the night, depriving it of its power and peril. It hurls a challenge to the wind and the rain, driving them into submission. It beckons the primitive and sophisticate alike to abandon their cares and their conceit and participate in the rites of workshop. It invites the heart of man to be restored, renewed, reborn – to leave behind forever his clouded vision, his distorted perception.

I am going blind, and I do not like it.

Sunlight. Moonlight. Starlight. Traffic light. Red on top. Green on the bottom. Red, green – O Rocky Road, tell me what you see. Tell me inside out, tell me upside down, tell me round the block, tell me round the town.

Today I went to school and a girl from Nova Scotia stopped me in the hall and said, "I'll read to you if you teach me Braille." Quietly, and with great control, I told her that I do not know how to read Braille. Please don't ask me to explain over and over again that I am not completely blind yet. Please don't ask me if I can see that sign over there. Please don't ask me if I can see the dust on your soul. Please don't ask me. Please don't ask me. Please don't ask me.

I think of those lovely lines by Dylan Thomas,

> "Do not go gentle into that good night ...
> Rage, rage against the dying of the light."

I wander down the boulevard of broken dreams, stabbing the pavement with my cane, piercing a path through the crowds with what is left of my vision. I am a sight. I have become one of the local characters that prowl along St. Lawrence Boulevard. I am too visible, a target for pity and abuse. I am too proud to admit that I am handicapped, too arrogant to identify myself as one of THEM.

I want to be lighthearted, lightfooted, lightheaded, trip the light fantastic. Instead I withdraw, hide my light under a bushel. As my vision deteriorates, my relationship to external reality changes and I turn inward to explore the inner landscape.

> The blue light of faith
> The red light of pleasure
> The white light of illumination
> The Guiding Light
> DIVINE LIGHT

They tell me I have tunnel vision in my right eye. Does that mean that I will better be able to see the light at the end of the tunnel? With my left eye, I see flashes of light, sometimes movement. I have been given a light sentence – only thirty years of darkness.

> Phosphorescent light
> Fluorescent Light
> Incandescent light
> Neon light
> Lights out

A well-meaning friend tells me a story about a blind man who can identify three hundred different types of shell by holding them in his hand. Is that all there is? Will I spend the rest of my days on some barren beach picking up shells and shouting their names to the dunes?

Oversimplifications are always a pleasure, for they make everything crystal clear for an instant before it fogs up again.
(Peg Bracken)

February 8

Have been up since 4 a.m. repotting the spider plants. Restless these days. I wake regularly at 4 or 5 in the morning and lie there doing a healing exercise that my father taught me – using the energy around me to supplement my own and focusing it on various parts of my body.

My eyes have become much worse. The good eye (the left) has had another bad bleed which has clouded my vision completely, so that I see only movement with it. I can see to a limited extent with my right eye – central vision only – and then just enough to allow me to function. No detail, no reading – except with difficulty with a magnifying glass.

It's been a heavy month for physical problems. Bad dose of the flu which left me exhausted and depressed and ten pounds lighter. Then a pap smear that came back with moderate cellular changes which may necessitate minor surgery. I start to feel like the end is closer than I thought, so I make a few decisions. Whether it is true or not is irrelevant.

I am working less in the book store. I spend three days a week there and three days a week at the Visual Arts Centre learning to make pots, both on the wheel and hand built. Debbie and Anna have offered me a space in their office that I could use as a studio when the course finishes in April. By then I hope to know some of the basics and will get myself a wheel. It is something that I can do without relying too much on visual information. Besides, I like to work with clay and I like its pliability.

So I spend more time with what I want to do and less time trying to earn a few extra dollars. Richard and I are planning to go to Greece this summer, with a stop in England first to visit the Harry Edwards Clinic where there is a group of psychic healers. My father thinks I should go to India. He has been reading books on Yoga. He says he would give me his eyes if it would help.

Have been having a whole series of psychic dreams. A few nights ago a child gave me a magic stone and I remembered while dreaming that someone else had given me this same stone before in another dream, and I asked the child where the stone came from. He said from a place in the mountain near "Bremmer," and there is a lake close by. I am beginning to feel that I have healing forces within me that need to find a way to be useful to me.

"I'm trying to find the balance between the light and the dark."
(Teresa Stratas, opera singer, in a film by Harry Rasky)

February 27

More crises. My kidneys are rapidly failing and it looks as if I will have to have a tube planted in my abdominal cavity to act as an artificial kidney to rid my body of toxic wastes. It is called peritoneal dialysis. This is all happening so suddenly; I have hardly had a chance to digest all this new information.

Richard and I are trying to plan our trip to Greece for April. The doctor says I may not even feel like going then and it may be a serious risk to my health.

Right now I am bargaining with the devil. I am buying time. I need to go to England to the Healing Clinic – not that I think I will be cured, but I need to go to reassure myself that I have done everything possible before I make an irrevocable decision and become dependent on an artificial kidney.

My life seems hopelessly tangled at the moment. I'm not sure which very serious aspect of it to deal with first. The most life-threatening situation is my kidneys, so that seems to have top priority. I wonder sometimes why I have to go on paying such a high price just for the privilege of continued life. I feel that I have paid my dues for at least several lifetimes, but somehow my debt never seems to be paid off. Even with this latest blow to my morale and whatever else is left for me to fight with, I know it doesn't stop there – that there is more to come. All I ask is that I be able to deal with whatever comes with some measure of grace and dignity.

March 16

Today I was declared legally blind. I feel strangely remote – not sad or surprised or relieved or even curious. Others around me seem to feel much worse than I do – the doctors, my relatives and friends. It seems to have something to do with facing one's own fears about mortality and the fragility of life.

Here I am, blind (though I still see enough to get around) and suffering from imminent kidney failure, and it's as if I am called upon to reassure them all that it's really not all that bad.

Life is not that important to me. I have come full circle from a week ago when I had a long conversation with Bill B. who has just become a father. Then I was full of hope and the possibilities for renewal. For the past few days the silence falls upon me as my world disintegrates relentlessly. I do little to arrest the process.

There is now nothing to look forward to – Richard tells me tonight that he really couldn't care less about a trip to Greece. I wonder now how I could have really believed it would happen. This dream I have had for years – I should have known better. Somehow it is harder to give up the dreams than anything else. The dream of raising a family, of traveling. I can hardly stand it. I wanted it all.

I notice that people turn away from me when I show my anger, depression, disappointment – like they can't stand to look their own fears and weaknesses in the face. They love me when I'm strong and full of shit, but show a little anguish and all of a sudden they bury their head in a book or close the door in my face. Too bad.

March 29

Two weeks ago they tell me I am legally blind. Today I pick up my camera for the first time in a year and discover that I can still make photographs. I guess I don't believe in other people's boundaries.

> *How many colours are there in a field of grass*
> *to the crawling baby unaware of "green"?*
> (Stan Brakhage)

April 14

Space shuttle "Columbia" has just landed after two days in space, traveling 25 times faster than the speed of sound, 176 miles from the earth's surface, completing 36 orbits – and I can barely get off the ground.

April 16

Thirty-eight years old.

Sitting on the bus on my way to work wondering why I am unable to make a decision about dialysis or kidney transplant or nothing. It has something to do with a lack of trust in the wonders of modern medicine and not wanting to be victimized by a treatment that may help alleviate one condition but could at the same time create another.

All the alternatives seem equally disagreeable if not dangerous and I seriously consider doing nothing and allowing nature to have its way.

I can understand and accept the process of dying better than I can cope with the uncertainty of medical intervention. I don't want to give anyone the power, or even the opportunity, to mess up my life. I want full responsibility for my life, my death. I do not want to blame anyone and if I choose badly, let it be my mistake and not someone else's ignorance or incompetence that causes me to suffer. The medical process of trying to keep me alive through some artificial means may save my life or merely prolong this earthly burden.

I am on a dangerous journey to the centre of myself. I am not at all sure that I will make it.

April 17

Rockburn. Driving through the mystical countryside, steel bridges rising stately into thin mist, well-traveled roads that disappear into the ephemeral fog. We the travelers, who slip gently between the silences, leave only an echo of our passage through this sweet realm.

May 22

Rockburn. A month later, same table, warmer evening; summer unfolds. I wear my favourite parrot shirt. We are again fed well. (Richard sings for his supper and mine, too.) All the beer and wine and whatever else we can handle. I have sworn to be prudent this time – so easy to be excessive when it's all for free. This indulgent night life has its price.

Just sitting here thinking how much I really like to hear Richard sing his music in these smoky bars – and how much the same music can drive me crazy in my house night after night.

Every time I come here, something ends up in my lap. Last time, Tom dumped a plate of food (a steak, no less). This time a shattered wine glass (empty, thank God).

I listen to the locals and their turn of phrase. They like Richard's hat (his five dollar Plattsburg special). "Hey, he's got a hat, eh, you got a hat; we should put 'em both on the back of the truck, eh. Drive 'em up to Shirley's Place and turn 'em loose. That'll teach 'em, eh?"

Quiet night at the Auberge. No rowdies about. Maybe they don't let them out until tomorrow night. I'm getting bored sitting here by myself, the wife of the entertainer.

Going to Vancouver for a month, if I can stay healthy that long. Decided to do some freewheeling before I undergo the operation ordeal. Just want to forget this cloud that looms over my shoulder. I live in the future these days, always concerned about what it will be like with a tube in my stomach, changing bags of fluid three or four times a day and all the rest of the crap I'll have to deal with.

When I can take it a day at a time, or even a few hours at a time, my life is more manageable. If I can deal only with the realities of the present instead of the imaginings of the future, I have a better chance at psychic survival. It is easy for me to be depressed these days. My physical and emotional energies are depleted and I need a great deal of rest. Some days I can't eat, due to nausea and worse. I have rediscovered vitamin B, which seems to help the nausea. I have several attacks of dizziness, lightheadedness and weakness in the limbs as well as some out-of-breath moments after climbing stairs.

I have forgotten what it is like to feel good except in rare moments.

What really disturbs me is that I have lost a lot of confidence in very simple things that I always took for granted. Things like walking. I am very shaky both because of my poor eyesight and my lack of strength. I can't trust my body to get me across the street in one piece. I am very unsure of myself in an unfamiliar place. I am learning to use my ears and my hands to guide me but I don't think I am going to make a very good blind person.

I treasure the sight I have left and do not want to give it up. It seems that my task in this life is to learn how to let go of many things. I wonder sometimes if I am equal to this karmic card I have drawn from a loaded deck. But then, the real issue is not how heavy is the load you get to carry through your life, but how you carry it. That's what it is all about. All I want is to be able to have some grace and dignity. Maybe that too I will have to give up.

I have dreams lately that I can see perfectly clearly as I ride through fields of multicolored flowers on a snowy white horse – flaming red poppies, delicious sun-yellow marigolds, soft orange zinnias, rose bushes with no thorns, dew-drenched morning glories climbing steadily toward the sky. I awaken in a state of euphoria, believing once again in visions and magic – and that is why I survive.

My father believes in the mystery. I need him to believe in the mystery when I no longer can, when the realities become too harsh. I think this strong feeling of being protected has come from him. Somehow he has always watched over me, even though there are things that he will never be able to protect me from. Still his spirit guides me though all the devils in Hades ride rampaging through the phantom night.

Well, the way I figure it, for whatever time that I have I will take it to the limit, for too soon all will belong to eternity.

June 6

St. Vincent de Paul Hospital, Brockville. Lying here listening once again to the night hawk and the familiar sound of trains rolling through the night in my childhood home town, reflecting on my life and what is left of it. Sick again, ending up in emergency here. I am better now, though weak. I think somehow that I felt that I had to suffer in my life to pay my dues and now it seems that I don't know how to do anything else – my suffering has become a habit! I wonder why I persist. I wonder for what great sin am I atoning?

June 7

Four in the morning. I sit here sleepless, drawing flowers and rediscovering the mystery, the magic of life. Everything in the universe is built of layers – the earth, plants, trees, even man-made things like buildings and even man himself. I want to paint a great waterfall of flowers.

July 8

Collapse in liquor store. They soaked an old towel in water (booze?) and gave it to me to cool off. "Do you want a doctor?" End up outside on park bench full of old men, vomiting my guts out.

Richard eats our whole spinach crop in one mouthful.

Every day brings new events. I force myself to be active, though I am extremely dizzy when I stand up or walk. I have been told that I am pregnant. Two tests have been positive. Dr. S. says there is about a five per cent chance that I can carry a child to full term. In all likelihood I will miscarry, but if there is any possibility of having this child I will do anything at all to ensure that it happens. It's really the only thing in the whole world that I want. I hesitate to ask the powers that be, "Why now? You could have picked a more appropriate time." My God, as I have said before, if there is a complicated way of doing things, I'll find it.

Yesterday, bright sunny day – the worst kind for me – white light, everything bleached so that I cannot see, cannot make distinctions, cannot see the edges. There is construction on the boulevard. I nearly fall into several dug-up pits, trip over barriers and end up standing in the middle of the intersection at Pine and St. Lawrence not knowing whether the light is red or green or which way it is to safety. I almost panic and start screaming but remember that it is against the law to hit a pedestrian. They impose heavy penalties for manslaughter. I pray very loudly amid the clamor of honking horns and a few obscenities and walk the straightest line I can into a red mailbox. God bless the Queen's Mail – that's the first time I've really been scared. I seriously consider the white cane. I think it's time.

I now call up Warshaw's with my grocery list and they deliver for me. The Portuguese grocer on the corner will also deliver anytime. Nice people.

I have found that so many people want to help. The worst feeling anyone can have is that of being helpless – they're all just dying to do something. I have a list a mile long. If anyone calls and asks, "What can I do?" I haul out the list and say, "Well, you have a choice of A or B or C or all of the above." I have finally lost my false pride and ask for help when I need it. I find I have a lot of friends ready, willing and able.

Odette is coming to read to me once a week in both English and French and to expand my acquaintance with French and Quebecois music. I look forward to it.

I can still embroider a little and am making a wall hanging (perhaps the beginning of a quilt) of birds and butterflies. It's small enough to carry around with me and so I bring it to the hospital to work on. I am in hospital for ten hours every Monday, Wednesday and Friday for the time being until I start to learn how to change the bags of fluid myself. Another week of this before they start to train me. I have a "toy" bag that I carry with me to amuse me during these ten hour stretches.

Coming out of local anesthetic – zylocaine – the same stuff the dentist uses to freeze gums to do dental work. Ears ring, mouth dry, and thick, numb tongue. Then like being very stoned – keep switching from one level of reality to another. One moment almost normal, then ZAP! I'm reading people's minds and controlling my environment – can foresee what will happen thirty seconds ahead. Spinning around, no physical strength, exhausted. I say, when the operation is not successful and they have to go into my stomach a second time to replace the catheter, "Forget the local (loco) anesthetic – put me out this time. I don't want to know a damn thing."

DAISIES

Listening to an interview of Debbie, the potter. She talks about having to make a choice: "What do I want to do with my life?" For me, too, it always comes back to that, and now more than ever there is a certain urgency. I do not want to waste my time in useless pursuits. Above all, I want to do something constructive, creative, something meaningful and positive.

July 9

Life is, above all else, miraculous.

Dr. S. (renal specialist) says that if I want to have this child they will do everything in their power to help me have it.

Well, I don't ask for much, but when I do, I ask for everything.

Dream. Climbing a high craggy mountain. Blue (my dog) is on another peak. I cannot reach him. I cannot climb down. There is a lady with a baby stroller who climbs down easily. I watch and wonder why I cannot. I decide to wake up. I've had enough.

Until we stop believing in power and possession, there can be no peace.
(K.T.B.)

July 10

Mina and Martha come for dinner last night to keep me company while Richard works late. Martha, who has no night vision (she has retinitis pigmentosa and will eventually be blind) and I stumble around and knock things over and Mina says, "I know why you invited me here. You want me to lead you two around and be your seeing-eye person." We all laughed ourselves silly.

Richard has been super through all this. I had such a hard time sharing my fears and disappointments with him until finally one night we sat at the kitchen table and I told him that when we were married I wanted a "normal" life with him, to raise a family and live like an ordinary person. I thought all I had to do was take my shot of insulin and watch my diet and everything would be okay. Then I started to go blind – and waited for months on end without getting pregnant. Then two miscarriages and now kidney failure. I told him that I never expected that things would work out like that and that most of all I did not want to be his sick wife and a burden to him. We both cried a lot.

I begin to realize now that it's okay to fall apart, that I don't have to be strong and invincible all the time. It feels good to lean on someone else for a moment, to reach out and say, "Hold my hand."

When I first found out that I would have to start dialysis or have a kidney transplant our friend Juan, who studied medicine for four years, said to me, "I won't give you any medical advice because it's not my place, but I will say you can consider yourself fortunate that at least you have time to get used to the idea before you have to make any irrevocable decisions. Think about the poor guy who is in a car accident and paralyzed for life. He hasn't got a choice. You at least have a choice." Wise words.

Terrible cramps last night – doubled up with pain. Am I aborting?

Dr. G. (gynecologist) comes to see me this morning and tells me the risks. Heavy conversation. And I say to him, "Of course you realize that it is impossible for me to make a rational decision. Even with all the information I have, in the end it will still be my emotions that decide. Rationally, I know it would be safer to terminate the pregnancy, but my heart would break and something in me likes the element of danger. I am frightened and exhilarated at the same time.

July 11

Saturday afternoon in the Alexis Nihon Plaza zoo. I've really overextended myself today. Grocery shopping, vacuuming the house, now a sidewalk sale. I buy three blouses and a white dress for $40 and am now ready to collapse. Debbie and I are going to see a film – pure escapism for the soul on a hot summer's day.

July 17

Helluva week. Tuesday at 8 a.m. it's back to the O.R. to have a fistula and the joining of a vein and an artery in my left arm – a backup system in case I have to switch to hemodialysis due to infection of the peritoneum or because of the pregnancy. Another local anesthetic – a nerve block to the left arm. Very strange sensation, as if my arm weren't there. I hit myself in the face twice when they asked me if I could lift my arm. I said, "Sure," and promptly let it drop on my head. Scary as hell. I insisted that they hold my arm after that and spent the next three hours holding on tightly to my hand with the other hand. Weird sensation of holding someone else's hand. The operation took three hours (usually takes one) and was not successful. The vein is blocked, so now I have to go through it all over again

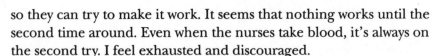

so they can try to make it work. It seems that nothing works until the second time around. Even when the nurses take blood, it's always on the second try. I feel exhausted and discouraged.

I am starting to learn how to do the exchanges (of peritoneal dialysis fluid) myself – not too difficult, but it will take some getting used to – carrying two liters of fluid around in my abdominal cavity for the rest of my life. That plus the fact that I have to wear the empty bag all the time around my waist is a nuisance and makes me look like the Goodyear Blimp or a Bartlett pear. Fortunately my weight is quite low to start with. My "dry" weight is fifty kilos (110 pounds); my weight with dialysis fluid is fifty-two kilos (115 pounds).

I fell apart the other night, yelling at Helen, one of the kitchen staff, over a dish of fruit salad. Nurse Carol started to get angry with me for reacting so much out of proportion to the situation. Helen was calmer. It was just all too much, these whole last few weeks. It had nothing to do with the fruit salad, of course, and both Carol and I ended up crying – me because I was falling apart and Carol because she felt badly for not being more sympathetic. I felt awful and later realized that just because I felt bad was no reason to make Helen feel bad too. I apologized and now she goes out of her way to feed me what I ask for.

Dr. A. (surgeon) says that his wife was bored after raising their three kids so got pregnant again, twice in one year. They now have two more kids: a boy, six who is heavy – they call him "Meat" – and a skinny girl, five, whom they call "Bones." I asked him if he had his white boots on during the operation. He reassured me that he did and I said, "That's good; now I can relax." White boots or not, the fistula still doesn't work. I wonder sometimes if all this is worth it. The novelty is wearing off. The honeymoon phase is over. Now it's just a daily drag, changing bags four times a day and having no strength or energy to do much in between.

July 18

Another crying jag last night due to cramps in stomach and pain in right shoulder and probable low blood sugar. Don't know if I can stand it. The thought of having to sit around for the rest of my life haunts me. Every time I move with all this fluid inside, it drives me crazy. And after I eat it's even worse. The dietitian, Karen, has given me a 2400 calorie diet to follow which I'll never manage. Baby or no baby, I'll be lucky if I can eat half of that. I feel so stuffed all the time that it's a wonder I have any appetite at all.

Today I feel a little better. Some days I can't talk to anyone, and feel very withdrawn. Today I am okay again after two or three days of depression.

Whatever else life is, it is a miracle. Pay your dues, do what you have to, but every so often it is necessary to stop and acknowledge the wonder.
(K.T.B.)

July 19

Home all day today and it becomes obvious to me that I have to get out of the hospital soon. I am becoming anesthetized, lying there lethargically watching the Saturday morning cartoons on TV and being hypnotized by the afternoon soap operas and re-runs. I fear brain damage before long. Time to move along and get it together.

July 30

I have an incredible sense of loss. Sometimes it hits me all of a sudden as I sit in this restaurant drinking my morning coffee. I am no longer pregnant and I feel the emptiness acutely. Being pregnant was such an affirmation of life, a counterbalance with the deterioration that is occurring in my body and threatening to destroy my very being. But alas, that tiny life-force could not continue to exist in the face of all those other denying forces.

I wonder if any of my dreams will come true. They seem such ordinary wants – health, a child – and yet so elusive. The pain of emptiness is far worse than any physical pain I have ever experienced. Richard's dream is to move to Nashville and make it in the music business. How can I tell him that it really doesn't matter, that perhaps the only thing of any importance is the relationships we have with others? Forget the fame and fortune, the elusive chase after the angels of the rainbow. We're all just passing through.

August 2

Kingston. My first trial weekend away – a trial run for the new bag system. I feel very vulnerable again, no longer protected by the safety and privacy of my own home. Here I am exposed, raw.

There is no answer. Seek it lovingly.
(John Ciardi)

August 7

Rockburn. Sounds of the country. The wind rushes through the tall maples, the harbinger of autumn sneaks through an attic window, the lamplight casts mysterious shadows across an empty chair, a rose bush blooms, a child sleeps in her mother's arms, a son returns home after his first week in the wide world, fresh bread and cheese and wine upon the round table. I want to be carried away by a great white bird who sings ever so softly and flies to the highest point.

October 20

The howling autumn leaves hurl themselves against the iron bars of winter. Summer fades – the last rose blown full and final.

October 28

La Cité. A real fall day with no sunshine. Cold and crisp, the kind of day I like. It has rained for two days straight after a glorious weekend in Kingston and a few wet days in Brockville. I am on the other side of deep depression again. I am starting to get used to the ebb and flow of my moods, floundering in the troughs, riding the crest until I crash on the rocks. I reach out often these days and always find someone there. So many have helped in so many ways; Debbie with her undaunted laughter, Juan with his sage advice, Bill F. with his riotous monologue on depression, and always Richard with his solid spirit like a mountain that never crumbles, my parents with their undying concern, Richard's parents with their warmth and sweet ways, Joan at the clinic with her humor and her convictions, Ann the dialysis unit chaplain with her smile and her ability to listen. And oh, so many others. George who calls all the way from Toronto to tell me not to despair, Anna who gives me a gorgeous fisherman's sweater to keep me warm, Mina who sends her mother's sturdy cane on a bus from London, Ontario, and complete strangers who pick me up when I fall or help me across the street when I am too scared to try to maneuver myself.

November 3

I walk through the streets of the city with my white cane and am not afraid. I fear most when I am behind closed doors. It does take courage to keep on opening those doors. Sometimes I don't have enough stubbornness to continue. Sometimes a gust of wind is enough to cause retreat. And sometimes I open the door wide in the midst of a raging blizzard.

November 8

My eyes are blind, my spirit broken as I try to grasp hold of some fleeting moment that will let me know that everything is still all right. I am lifeless these days, no desire, no passion, only passive non-acceptance of my fate. I seem to be digging in deeper and deeper as the winter approaches.

Yesterday, the first snowfall. Today I slip on the ice. Richard says my spirit is not broken – only wounded.

November 22

I am not inspired these days – barely alive at all. Richard is the only one who sustains me. We talk and grow close together, just at a time when it would seem that we should be farthest apart, our external lives full of uncertainties. It is all so strange, this life. We get along and love each other very much, but we have no passion for each other – are we just comfortable old friends? I can offer him nothing but my suffering; he offers me life and renewed strength. I need him and a normal relationship. I need his family and their strong ties. My own family which I also need is more neurotic, more crazy and anxiety provoking.

I choose between life and death. I am barely hanging on by an ever so slender thread. Richard says there is no threat to our relationship, that he will always care for me, that the real threat is not anyone else, but his desire, be it music or whatever. He has dreams and I want him to follow his dream to the end. He has worked so hard to try to realize it and I will not stand in his way with my suffering – he wouldn't let me stand in his way anyway. His desire to make something of his talent is the best part of him. He is taking the risk. We are both taking a risk. Will it lead to more life? Or further complexity.

... And isn't that what we are all looking for — to find a decent way to live with some sort of honesty, some sort of dignity, without taking too much of a toll of each other's lives?
(K. T. B.)

December 7

I am so very vulnerable right now. It doesn't take much for me to fall apart. I stay in bed most of the day. For days on end I can seem to find no purpose, no reason to get up.

If it weren't for Richard and his patience and care I don't know what I would do. His music is the only lively thing around here. Friends, too, drop by with words of encouragement, and my mother at seventy-six has come all the way to see me for a few days. I'm not much good to anyone these days – it will take time before I am ready to face anything again. I don't want to be a burden to myself and I torment myself saying I ought to be stronger and quit this self-pity. But I can't quite manage it yet.

I try to get dressed every day even if it is not until 5 p.m. Yesterday I had a bath and washed my hair for the first time in three weeks. Last weekend we went to spend two days in the country with Bill and Susan. Gradually I am getting better. Maybe I'll get Mother to help me put up the Christmas tree – THAT would be something!

I dream about finding a purpose, a meaning for my life. That I must do if I am to survive.

December 9

Odette and I talk about innocence and the pot of gold at the end of the rainbow. We are the believers who see no wrong in illusion, who drift through the midnight world and catch moonbeams in outstretched arms. We are the hope of the weary and downtrodden; we are the spirit of life and its lovers. We reap the rewards and hazards of our meager existence; we replenish the well when it is dry. We fabricate lives that constrict and bind us to temporal phantoms. Who gives me the right to deny my life? What right do I have to call down the shades of darkness just because my small light is fading? Rise up! Rise up! And seek for pearls and rubies even though it seems that all is merely glass.

December 12

Alone again tonight – the most difficult time. I try to trick myself by making little things for me to do – bake Christmas cake, wash hair, rinse out a blouse, make chili. But through it all, I am lonely and anxious about being alone. I call my friends just to make contact, I take sips of Cointreau and wish that I could drink myself into oblivion without getting sick. I remember when Richard and I first met and used to go out on a Saturday night, then come home and make love till the early hours. I remember and feel the ache of empty arms. I cannot fill up the emptiness. My only chance for survival is to start to care about myself. I cannot depend on Richard to fill up my life any more. I need him, I need to care for him and I need to let him go. He says he will always come back and I believe him.

I think about women whose men have gone to war and have been away for weeks, months, even years and I think it would be easier to see Richard leave than to watch him come and go to another woman. And yet to her, Carole, I too am the "other woman" with whom she has to share her man. I have him most of the time but I feel that his heart is elsewhere. I hope that Richard will have the courage to admit his leanings and follow his heart. I feel that I am his wife, an obligation, a kind of comfortable, familiar warmth that no longer invites passion.

I want to be a woman again, not a passive partner in a lukewarm relationship. I want to be carried away, transported by love, by loving and being loved. I want to be transformed by the unity of love. I want to melt into his arms and be free to fly together above the clouds where the sun always shines. I want to explore the depths of his soul. I want to be part of his world, part of his life. My purpose is to see him happy and content, and if I am not able to do that then I must allow him the freedom to find that elsewhere.

I suffer for my love for him – my love for him at times makes me happy. Mostly, however, I long for his touch, his warmth, his smile. I wanted to give him a child but that was not to be and I feel a profound sense of failure. I don't think it would have made any difference in our relationship. Yet I still wanted to give him the gift of life even though it might have meant giving up my own life to do so. I cannot think of any other gift so precious. Tonight I cannot even think what to give him for Christmas. Perhaps I can only give him his freedom to live his life to the full regardless of my feelings. Still, my feelings are important too, and it is only part of me that is willing to share my husband, my love with another woman.

I don't think I will be able to sleep tonight. If only I could find some rest. I am exhausted in my heart. It beats so strongly and aches so much; the pain will not dissolve, there is no relief. Why do

I allow myself to suffer so much? Why can't I just get on with my life? I keep feeling that I will die soon so it doesn't matter anyway, and yet I have to believe that I will live for a while at least. I'm just not sure what to do with my life. I am not sure what will keep me going. Sometimes it is merely the daily routine. Sometimes I need more. Mostly I need more. I am having difficulty finding a reason to live, a purpose. It has to start with a will to live, with the desire to take care of myself. I hope that is enough – I need to relearn how to be alone with myself and how to recreate my life.

December 15

Bill and Susan's – feel a new surge of life within me. Begin to feel that there is yet a chance for survival, that my spirit wakes after weeks of slumber. I wonder what this new cycle will bring. I wonder what I will be able to bring to it. I have to learn to make space for myself.

September 29, 1982

Paul tells us a story at dinner the other night. "I used to always burn my mouth on the oatmeal my mother served me for breakfast when we were kids. Then one day my father said to me, 'You have to start from the edge, where it's cooler.' At that moment, I knew that my father knew everything."

Eggplant and Tomato Casserole
(From a PBS TV program)
Eggplant (sautéed) layered with fresh sliced tomato, mozzarella cheese and onion and basil. Cover and bake at 375° for 40 minutes.

October 5

Feel so vulnerable with this cane – so conspicuous. Even the taxi drivers are starting to recognize me. I used to like the anonymity of sinking into the back seat of a cab, to be carried silently through the streets. No longer. Now they have either picked me up before and therefore feel free to be familiar or see the cane and get protective. The cane also acts as a magnet for all the loonies in town. This guy comes up to me at the bus stop and says, "Going home?" No reply. "Going out?" No reply. Then, "What happened to your leg?" "That is none of your business!" He gives me the finger and stomps off. To some people I am fair game for any kind of interference. It annoys me and makes me uncomfortable. I don't like being a target.

Autumn descends. It is fair and clear.

January 12, 1983

Notes for a speech to medical students at the Montreal General Hospital regarding a patient's view of dialysis:

- Without the will to live, no amount of medical technology can keep the patient alive
- Important for the physician to believe in power of body to heal itself and believe in miracle of life
- Fine balance between denial and acceptance
- Go through stages of anger, denial, acceptance, bargaining. Never leave any of those stages behind. They recur frequently.
- Importance of relationships – "the need to be needed" – necessity of maintaining self-worth, of being important to someone else
- Easier to be a part-time dialysis patient than a full-time one
- Art of healing – the importance of touch
- Losing the dream, when you have no energy, no strength, no desire
- Other patients are part of the team too – we watch each other, provide support, protection
- No matter what you tell the patient, no matter how much information you give them, you can never really prepare them ...

July 20

It is 2 a.m. and I am embarked upon another sleepless night. Water is still dripping off the roof after a heavy rain. The smell of charred wood spills through the air, fire trucks drone on the boulevard nearby – another fire in the neighbourhood. We are secure for the night. I sit and consider what has happened to me in the last two years. What has changed, what has remained the same, what is in transition? How am I these days? How do I spend my time? Who and what am I connected to?

There is much that is changed. I have discovered a few secrets, come to terms with much that is stressful in my life, redefined my priorities and thrown out some attitudes that are of no use to me.

I have begun to learn that it is not so much what I do that is important but what I am, and I have had to separate the two of necessity. There was a time not so long ago when I could do nothing due to my illness and severe depression. I lost my will to do anything at all; I lost my dreams, my hopes, my self-respect.

I had been so tied up, so identified with my ability to do, to accomplish, to succeed that when I was no longer able to do even the simplest task I collapsed inside. My very identity became so threatened that I almost lost it completely. Gradually things changed and I realized that I could do simple things – ordinary things like take a bath, walk half a block, get up in the morning. All those things that I had always taken for granted now became the most crucial, most essential accomplishments. Now I can do much more but it is still often the simplest tasks that give the most pleasure. I have learned to put more trust in what I am than in what I can do.

It is important not to let your illness, your handicap, your limitation define your life. You have to learn to use that limitation to broaden your horizons. There are things that have happened to me in the last two years that would never have taken place if I had not experienced physical and emotional turmoil. If I had been able to see properly it would never have occurred to me to advertise for volunteer readers to come to the hospital and read to me on dialysis. I would have never entered into relationships with Juan, Marlene, Nancy, Jean-Claude, Genevieve. Matthew would probably not have made over a hundred tapes for me. The list is endless.

I keep forgetting that my body doesn't know how to build up strength – that I have to start from zero almost every day.

I am awkward with people. I don't know how to *be* anymore. I feel "different," as if everyone else knows how to lead a normal life except me. I marvel at ordinary things – people shopping, taking care of children, gossiping on street corners, riding the bus. I do all these things, too, but I have this feeling all the time I am doing them that it is all rather extraordinary – as if I don't quite belong with the rest of the crowd. I think I have spent a lot of energy in my life trying to feel comfortable with the ordinary. In fact, I feel more at ease in out-of-ordinary states. I look for the marvelous and the strange.

July 31

Fortieth anniversary party for Richard's parents at his brother's place. Debbie and I did a family tree for them. Brennan tree to follow.

It has been very hot all day. Now it is three in the morning and a gentle rain falls. I think of camp and wish that I could be there to watch the sunrise. I do healing exercises to give myself some positive energy. I wonder why I have to struggle so, why everything I do is so difficult. I am tired; I am tired of having no energy, tired of being so self-absorbed. I'm looking for a change in my life, and at the same time I resist change. The familiar way of being is so comfortable.

I am so good at being sick it frightens me. I have learned to cope too well. But now I feel that all those nameless terrors that I am usually able to keep hidden, under control, are about to burst through, rise to the surface and disrupt the delicate balance.

I feel as if I were in a house like in a horror movie and outside stalks some unknown force that has its arms and legs already through the doors and windows. I'm not sure if it is friend or foe, only that I cannot keep it from breaking in much longer. I am curious and afraid at the same time. I want to do something foolish, something mad. I long for a few moments of oblivion.

I think about a night in Lighthouse Park, Vancouver: George, Matthew and I. We lit a match and I said, "You will be the first to forget" (to George), "You will be the last to remember" (to Matthew), "and I will be left holding the match" (to me).

I await another sunrise. I lie quietly counting raindrops, wondering why the back yard does not fill up with water and drown us all. Somehow the rain is absorbed into the soil, it makes things grow, we do not drown, we are only a little wet for a while. Soon the sun will rise, another night forgotten, fading into the crystal clarity of early morning. The rain will stop, the earth will absorb and absorb and absorb and give back fruit and blossoms.

I've got my freedom but I don't have much time.
(Rolling Stones)

August 31

Have been feeling so much better this last month. My strength and energy have finally returned after a two-year struggle. So I have survived the struggle – so what now? I have survived – but for what?

It now becomes a question of what do I do with this life that has been given back to me. There is a responsibility for me to do something with that life. In many ways dialysis is now more difficult. The pain is still the same – but it is more difficult to bear. I am less tolerant, more impatient and more afraid that something will go wrong and I will be flat out again. I have nothing really to complain about and yet I complain all the time. It seems that the stronger I become, the more irritable and impatient I am. A great deal of my renewed energy is burnt up in negative states.

Graham (psychiatrist) tried to tell me today that I was depressed, that I was suffering. I practically threw him out of the room (except that I was at a disadvantage, tied down to the machine). He was trying so hard to help me when I didn't need help. The relationship has changed. I am stronger, more brittle, and I react angrily to gratuitous hand outs. The sin of pride. The price of self-respect. As my energy increases, not only does the positive become more apparent but also the negative.

Isolation: December 20 to January 11
December 20

In hospital (gangrene of middle left toe). I dream last night that Susan throws baseballs at me and hits me three times in the head.

Today I am afraid of the pain. For the moment there is none, but from all I hear of gangrene, it is extremely painful. And since it may take as long as six months for the toe to dry up and drop off, I may be in for a long winter.

I know there are ways of controlling pain other than with drugs. I need some training before the pain becomes unbearable.

Richard is bringing my portable typewriter today so I can begin working.

You will understand that all these obstacles are very useful to a man. If they did not exist, they would have to be created intentionally, because it is by overcoming obstacles that man develops those qualities he needs.
(George Gurdjieff)

January 10, 1984

Some books are meant to be read aloud. My father has been reading Shirley MacLaine's latest, called *Out on a Limb*, and we have spent the afternoon exploring the realms of esoterics and cosmic connections. My father remembers childhood experiences, forgotten intimations of untravelled roads, of scattered threads left unwoven into the carpet of his life. He talks and tries to weave it all

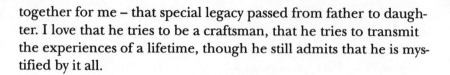

together for me – that special legacy passed from father to daughter. I love that he tries to be a craftsman, that he tries to transmit the experiences of a lifetime, though he still admits that he is mystified by it all.

January 15

Destiny, super efforts and keeping in shape physically – using unaccustomed movements, postures, gestures, as a means to changing habitual patterns.

Everything in the universe is in motion. Nothing remains the same forever or ceases to exist.

We are only just beginning to learn about computers. Is mankind too part of some larger computer, programmed, destined, doomed?

January 16

I no longer have to spend all my energy on survival; there is some left over. So the question becomes what to do with that energy. Right now I am being very indulgent in thinking that I will write a book. It could go either way – towards discipline or indulgence.

January 17

I lose so much energy when I am outside. Everything takes my attention.

I am not so much afraid of dying as I am of having to live without options.

Sometimes the hardest thing to deal with in chronic illness is the attitude of the people around you – particularly those closest to you.

January 20

We are open to new experiences when out of our normal state through illness, drugs, work.

The writing is neither discipline nor indulgence. It has become an obsession.

He works most when he appears to be doing nothing.
(James Kirkup, "The Poet")

January 25

I talk to empty elevators, hold conversations with people I don't recognize (because I can't see them clearly) and take photographs of people who are no longer in the frame – in my mind they are still in the photograph. I wonder if I have taken enough photographs with my mind to have a storehouse of images available, if and when I can no longer see.

I've gone through lyricism, romanticism, and mysticism to the realization that it is only through hard work that you get anywhere at all.
(K.T.B.)

January 27

Fractured vision – is this why I write and think in fragments?

Not everyone who carries a white cane is totally blind. Not all sighted people can see clearly. Not everyone who is blind carries a white cane.

Card from John R. – "You weren't meant to spend your life sitting on a bedpan. Get well soon."

Me: "I didn't feel like coming to dialysis this morning."

John (technician in dialysis unit): "Why didn't you call in sick?"

Much laughter ...

I should write a pamphlet for dialysis patients who are considering a transplant and call it, "To pee or not to pee."

One of the secrets of writing is to learn what your work habits are and what are the things that keep you from working. When you know how your work/nonwork cycle operates it is easier to outsmart laziness or distractions or all the other priorities in which we allow ourselves to indulge (and which keep us from our work).

Still busy trying to be heroic – which is to say that I am trying to get on with my ordinary life. In this realization (that of trying to be heroic), perhaps I am also admitting that though I can't slay *all* the dragons in the world, at least perhaps I can learn not to create any more.

January 29

Seeing clearly is not always a question of good eyesight.

Dream last night – only a fragment. There is a car. It explodes and burns – charred black – but through the frame of the car I can see that my suitcases and valuables are still intact inside the car. I interpret this as meaning that no matter what the external circumstances of my life, even the most hazardous, it is still possible to stay intact inside. The body(car) can fall apart, but the things necessary for the "journey" (the suitcases) may still be there untouched by disaster.

I woke up sweating and very cold.

February 1

I have learned to treat my body, my physical condition like a demanding child always tugging at my sleeve for attention. My first impulse is to say, "Go away. Don't bother me now. I don't want to have to stop what I am doing to pay attention to you." Then I realize that it will go on demanding my attention until I listen to it. So I give it my full attention, then say, "Okay, you've had your share. I've taken care of your needs. Now it's time for the rest of me, so give me a break and let me get on with my life."

We all have things to learn from each other. I don't think it is accidental that we know the people we do. Sometimes I look around me and wonder what I could possibly learn from this or that person. Then all of a sudden a door opens and I see clearly what it is.

Leoni and I are talking about lunch. She says it's terribly cold downstairs in the locker room where she has hers. "That's not reality," she says, "It's too cold, cold, cold."

"Where's reality, Leoni?"

She answers, "I don't know – I'm still looking for it. It's not down there, though. It must be somewhere warm."

February 2

My answer to that frequent comment, "You have a lot of courage": to them I say no, courage is always a matter of choice – of risking one's life for another person or principle. No, it is hardly courage, for the situation has been thrust upon me. No, what I do have is a certain determination to live a full life. It is a matter of building a fortress to which I can retreat, where I can recover from the next bombardment. The fortress is not an external structure, but rather an internal state that can withstand the onslaught no matter what.

I am building a fortress.

When I step from the darkness into the light, I have to pause for two or three minutes until my eyes adjust to the brightness.

They no longer respond automatically. In those few moments of stillness I have a chance to come to a full stop in the midst of my daily routine. A time to remember myself as I wait to see where I am and where I can safely step next.

Homeopathy – the process by which substance is reduced and refined to its purest essential ingredients – concentrated form of energy. I write the way I talk – repeating myself, explaining myself over and over to make sure the point is understood. I overwrite, I suffocate the listener, I leave no room for the reader to make his own connections and conclusions. How to make simple the complexity? (The "kiss" treatment – keep it simple, stupid?) Or how to say the same old thing in a fresh way.

Curry
(recipe from Martha Shea)

lentils	1/4 tsp. mustard, cayenne
oil, 2 Tbsp.	1/2 tsp. coriander
2 cloves garlic, crushed	salt, pepper
1 tsp. cumin, turmeric	onion, tomato

February 7
I am in danger of drowning most of the time. Sometimes the only thing that keeps my head from going under is my curiosity about what is happening around me.

February 16
My eyes have been blurring all day. It disturbs me to think that I may be interrupted again. It seems my life is a constant series of interruptions.

Is it possible to go in one direction for any length of time? Is it possible to do anything at all? I feel that I am always fighting the laws of inertia, of gravity, like some sort of Don Quixote battling planetary laws instead of windmills. Am I wasting my time, my energy?

I do not feel that I have the right to pass judgement of how anyone chooses to live his life, just as I do not feel anyone has the right to tell me how to live mine.

February 22
It is impossible to live our lives in a straight line. There is a basic narrative structure to our daily existence but it is constantly inter-

rupted by intrusive sounds, repeated images, fragments of conversation, memories of the past, associations with the present, dreams for the future, stray thoughts, the demands of ourselves and others. There are moments of illumination, interludes of darkness, periods of pain – always something that requires our attention and makes it impossible for us to continue in any one direction for very long.

Perhaps it is these interruptions rather than our desired direction that form the very heartbeat and substance of life. Perhaps after all it doesn't matter which road we follow as long as we ask the right questions along the way.

Life is like trying to nail jello to the wall.
(TV commentator)

February 23

My father calls, deeply depressed, questioning his self-worth. I listen and wonder what I can say or do to relieve his burdens. There is very little that I can do except to listen, to offer my support and acknowledge that it's okay for him to feel the way he does. He wants to hide his feelings, especially from me, thinking that he has to be a source of strength for me at all times. I tell him that it's natural to feel the way he does when he gets so little positive reinforcement.

Both my parents need the same thing and it is the one thing they are unable to give to each other. Their situation has become quite desperate.

February 24

I wonder sometimes if we don't learn more about ourselves when we are off the path, the road (or whatever metaphor one wishes to use) than when we are on it. It seems to me that I spend more time in the ditch than I do on the road and that rather than waste my time and energy trying to figure out why I fell off the road or how to get back on, I would do better to explore the ditch. After all, that is where I spend most of my time and as such it seems wiser and more profitable to start from where I am rather than from where I would like to be. By understanding the nature of the ditch and why I fell into it in the first place, I have a better chance to get out of it – and a better chance to learn something about myself and my propensity for ditches. The road cannot teach me any of that – it only provides a reference point, a stabilizing influence, a structure from which to get my bearings as I struggle along with my burdens and my dreams.

If your mind is ordered, the more information you have, the more understanding. If your mind is disordered, the more information you have, the more confusion.

Pesto (Sauce for Pasta)
1/2 c. olive oil   4 cloves garlic
1 c. basil leaves   1/2 c. romano cheese
parsley to taste
Blend in blender. Serve over pasta.

March 4

I feel like a bank being "cased" by a bunch of bandits planning a robbery. I feel as if all my safety deposit boxes have been hauled out of the vault and lie scattered in the street.

I am tired of being the lamb led to the slaughter. As the story goes, the lamb is always saved at the last minute. I sometimes think that it would have been better if I had been slaughtered the first time around. Instead I have to repeat this cycle over and over again, dying piece by piece. I hate this relentless deterioration – my pancreas, kidneys, eyes and now my toes. I hear the wings of vultures overhead. I see Sisyphus pushing a large boulder up a steep hill only to have it roll back down when he reaches the top. Was the going up worth the coming down? Sisyphus and I – the boulder grows larger as we grow weaker and smaller, but not weak or small enough to be crushed by the rock. Sisyphus and I always have just enough strength to push our boulders to the top but not enough strength to keep it there for long.

The law of gravity is irrefutable – and yet birds fly and man has gone to the moon.

What is the privilege of the dead? To no longer have to die.
(Jean-Luc Godard, *Alphaville*)

March 11

I am only as strong as the support systems I have around me. The doctors, nurses and staff who look after me physically, school that looks after my mind, Richard who looks after my heart, my parents and the government who look after me financially. I must be a great drain on them all – with so little of myself to give in return.

I feel an imminent sense of loss. It started ten days ago when I lost my wedding ring, an eighty-five year old treasure that belonged to Grandmother Taylor. Now I am about to lose a couple of toes. I am afraid I will not be able to finish my courses and will lose fifteen credits and a whole year's work.

Once upon a time I was falling in love. Now I'm falling apart.
(Dolly Parton)

Isolation: March 26 to April 3
March 30

Two dreams. Richard and Bob and I are in a rowboat that is rapidly sinking. I manage to climb out onto the dock. They disappear under the dock and eventually reappear on the other side of the dock. They yell at me, "Why didn't you tell us we were going under the dock?" I tell them that I cannot see. They don't hear me because they keep bobbing up and down in the water. I yell louder but still they do not hear me. Bob keeps pushing Richard's head under till he is gasping for breath. I am frantic on the dock. (This dream occurred the night after surgery.)

In the second dream, I have three black toes. I peel off the layers of blackness and find three healthy new toes underneath. (This dream happened several days after having two toes amputated.)

"Looking us over for fair."
(Mother – translation: looking carefully at us)
"To get the march on."
(Mother – translation: to get the jump on)

April 10

My universe expands once more. The less I see, the more I have to focus (my eyes, my attention, my life).

It is necessary to identify my needs; I need fuel to burn constantly, now that I know that it is easier for me to go out there to find it instead of waiting until it haphazardly finds me.

If my body would just leave me alone for a while I could do something with my life. In the meantime I steal moments.

April 11

How strange it is knowing that I could walk away so easily. I should go home but I'm not sure any more where home is. It is not where I thought it was.

May 7

I have been traveling far into the night. It is dark and I have lost my way for a time. I wait impatiently for the returning of the light and when it comes, it is always too bright for me. Now I am weary and cannot rest. I am worn down with "being tiredness." I feel sometimes that I must have been burnt out at fifteen and have been some sort of energy parasite ever since, feeding off other people's batteries. I think I pulled the plug on myself long ago.

There was a time when I thought it must be wonderful to be able to fly. Now I think it would be wonderful just to be able to walk more than a few blocks without tiring or experiencing such excruciating pain in my leg and foot.

June 5

My mother told me there'd be days like this – and I believed her. But I never thought that the days would become weeks and months and years.

Isolation: June 19

July 3

It seems there are two types of relationships – one that says if it hadn't been for you, I'd have been able to live my life the way I wanted, the other if it hadn't been for you I'd have never accomplished the things that I did.

Surgery — amputation — left leg below the knee: July 13

July 24

Eighth anniversary. Starting to feel better. Everyone is so good to me. I walked a few steps with the walker but have very little strength.

This pen is better. Can't see the other one too well. Time to get interested in the outside world again. I begin to reach out for those I love. I cry easily and am overwhelmed by the many kindnesses people have shown me.

Memories: how pleasant to recall.
The only paradise from which we may never be driven.
(Paul Margolf, Betty's neighbour)

July 26

Richard took me out today – over to the Royal Vic Hospital. Dad is there – he broke his hip a week ago when he and Mother arrived in Montreal. He looks so frail and tentative. He talks about camp. We hold each other's hands. He is so dear to me.

My mother and I have spent many precious hours together, talking, laughing. Mother rubs my back, my legs, and brings delightful gifts and her own special warmth. Betty came this morning all the way from the Adirondacks. She is like a sister and always enriches my life.

Richard's parents were here last night – they, too with their support and care. Richard, my true love, whom I adore and could not live without. Martha, my friend who sends me flowers and makes me laugh. Joy and Mary Jane, old friends who send letters of remembrance. And Debbie, my sister-in-law who talks to me when I am bored and lonely and tells me funny stories. And oh so many more.

July 29

Richard, my love, who cares for me and takes me outside in a wheelchair so that I can feel the ground under my foot and feel the summer breeze in my hair. He is so good to me.

July 30

More cards and letters from Marianne and Joan W. – nurses from other floors who remember me and drop in to see me – Richard's cousin Fred and Leslie, his Aunt Mary of whom I am very fond.

I watch a program on how to deal with change – main point is that one's essential worth is not dependent on external circumstances.

July 31

Have had many dreams in hospital, most of which I cannot remember. One in particular I do recall, in which I am with my Indian guide high up on the top of a mosque or some other church. He tells me that I should not be up there (in such a precarious position?) and then shows me the city below with a broad sweep of his hand as if to show me all the possibilities. I am not afraid of being up there and I am also assured that I will be able to get back down to the ground.

August 1

Wonderful visit from Bill and Susan. Richard arrived too, and they all took turns baby-sitting Samantha (age three) in the car outside. Letters from Hilda (marvelously written) and my childhood friend Carole, whom I have seen only once (at Queen's) since I was twelve. It amazes me. People just seem to come out of the woodwork. I guess that is part of the beauty of growing up in a small community.

My hand feels stronger tonight. I feel stronger in general. Yesterday I was sick all day and night – anxiety at what the future holds, mostly. Today I am more confident.

Called Mary and she as always offers reassurance and encouragement. A woman who says what she thinks and feels so that I always know where I stand with her. She tells me about her friend Mildred who has worn a prosthesis for years and gets around just fine, as I am sure I will too. Also talked to John (cousin) whose life has been turned upside down due to a separation from Deborah. They are starting counseling next week and John seems hopeful that something positive will come of it. I hope so – they are both such good people, stubborn and proud as many of us are – vulnerable and fragile too.

My lovely mother calls, worried about my being so sick yesterday. Today is another day and I reassure her. It was such a treat when she was here. We so rarely have a chance to spend time together. This time we spent many wonderful intimate moments. She is such a strong person. She has amazing resilience and energy. I feel that I have never really had the chance to know her and am just beginning to have that opportunity. It means the world to me. I am overwhelmed by how fortunate I am to have such remarkable relatives and friends.

The only time I am at ease with myself is when I am writing.
(Tennessee Williams)

Rose

August 4

Have been typing letters all afternoon. Like Tennessee Williams, I am only at ease with myself when I am writing. Physically it is becoming more and more difficult to write by hand or typewriter. Neuropathy seems to be slowly affecting my hands. I have two fingers which are uncomfortably numb on my left hand. I don't seem to have anything very stirring to write anyway. I have said it all in my letters. I think sometimes I tell the same story over and over – maybe with a few refinements.

August 5

Bad dream. Dreamt that friends came to the house and Richard did not wake me because he was embarrassed about my being a cripple. I woke up and found a baby in my arms and went out to see the two couples who were visiting and gave the baby to its mother. Then I went to the 'fridge to find it full of bottles of milk that they had brought for us, each labeled with the percentage of milk and cream. Then they left and I screamed at Richard for being embarrassed about me and not waking me up. I woke up crying. Funny, because we spent such a good day together at home.

I realized later after last night's dream that pain has to find a way out. Physical pain is felt in the body. Emotional pain is more complex and often I am made aware of it through my dreams. Gabrielle (nurse) gave me a wonderful massage to calm me down after last night's dream. It worked and I slept well.

August 11

Disappointed that I can't get out of the hospital to go to the family reunion in Kingston – the annual event of the Richardson clan and Grandma Brennan. My stump is infected and is showing signs of further gangrene which may mean more surgery. Richard is staying here too. We had planned to stop in Brockville to see Mother and Dad.

Dad says he must have been in a daze while in the Royal Vic. Sometimes, especially with older people, with the combination of anesthetic, drugs for pain and the shock of a broken hip, a person can get very disoriented. Dad thought we (Mother, Dad, Richard and I) were on a boat going up the Saguenay River to see the white whales. Now I remember that he said (while in hospital) that he felt like a beached whale and once while I was talking to him, he said he was having a whale of a time! He also thought we were all dead and then I came to him and said, "You still have me, Dad." The stories of his "travels" go on and on. I'm trying to get him to put it all on tape.

We were all so worried, thinking he had gone over the edge permanently. It is a relief to hear him sounding normal again. Graham (psychiatrist) kept trying to tell me that it was probably only temporary. Fortunately for all of us he was right.

Betty has called several times and been a great comfort to me and supportive. She tells me about her network of friends, all of whom know about me and who are sending me good vibes. Chloe who called after my surgery said, "Don't call it phantom pain, call it phantom sensation." I knew immediately why Betty feels Chloe is a special person. I liked her right away. And Betty's friend Rana who is blind and to whom Betty has read parts of one of my diaries. Betty and I have grown closer these last few years. Our experiences vary widely; our hearts are close together. We are sisters-in-heart.

It is now 10 p.m. This is the chronicle of a day – feelings, thoughts, recollections, hopes, dreams, realities. I measure my life in moments – each one of them precious, each one of them unique.

I have a lot to answer for. By that I mean that I feel that people sometimes look to me for answers. I always say, "Look inside yourself." There are few who know how to do that.

August 12

Throwing up again off and on all day. Slept all morning. Visit from Joan O. who used to read to me on dialysis to help me with my courses. She's from Newfoundland, adopted, ex-alcoholic and one of the nicest people I've ever met. She brought me a whole bag of wool to keep my fingers busy. Martha S. dropped in before supper on her way to see her sister Dianne who has been in India studying for three years. Martha has been a great friend to me these last couple of years. She gave me the keys to her apartment and I used to go there after dialysis on Fridays for a change of scene and tea and a chat. Sometimes we had supper together – mostly eggs and toast or Indian curry. She saved my life when I was in the deep blues. She's studying to be a lawyer. Then a phone call from my old friend Joy in Brockville, whom I have known since I was eight. She is planning to come to Montreal on the 23rd to see me. Richard said he had a wonderful conversation with my parents last night. At the end Dad said, "God bless you." I have such warm, wonderful friends and family.

I have been in hospital for almost two months. I can't remember what it feels like to walk around freely. Strange how quickly the body and mind adapt to new circumstances. I still feel as if my foot were there – sensations and early morning cramps.

August 13

Dream. I can feel my left leg and foot. I look down and they are both there. I walk around and say, "Get Dr. B. and show him that I'm better." I am terrified it will disappear again. I awake crying. Dr. S. tickles my right foot to wake me up and I tell him my dream. He says that it's common to have those kinds of dreams. It seems the body adapts before the heart and mind.

Betty is coming on Thursday, Joy on the 23rd; a rose from Mary and Bob, a card from Mother – my "network," the people who support me. Also a note from Chloe, a visit from Ann and Mavis and my three doctors. Things look a little more hopeful today.

The worrisome black patch on my stump is drying out but it may take a long time to heal. I think I'm going slightly nuts from restlessness, boredom and lack of physical activity. I'm starting to act like a loony, bouncing up and down in the bed, touching my toes, scratching my head and twisting around every which way. I have my crocheting, typewriter, quilt, etc. But it's not enough. I need to get out of here.

I watch the clock, I watch TV, I crochet, I work on my quilt, I write, I take sleeping pills to knock me out and I take Demerol for pain and oblivion. I hope I will fall asleep, yet I can't sleep all the time. Somehow the time passes. I watch the clock, I watch TV, I crochet, I work on my quilt – the endless cycle. Is this life? Is that all there is?

A lot of how you think about things
starts with where you wake up in the morning.
(Jack Troy, potter, quoted by Betty K.)

August 14

Today I feel a sense of accomplishment. Who is to say why today is different than yesterday? I'm thinking of the quotation that our perception of the world often depends on where we wake up in the morning. I interpret that it is not so much "where" in terms of our external surroundings as it is our internal state. My "innards" have been in better shape today. That's the difference.

My quilt is coming along well and I have started to crochet Richard's scarf – red, blue, orange, yellow and pink. I am pleased with it so far.

A Persian violet from Debbie's parents, Phyllis and Johnny, phone call from my parents. Richard, faithful as always, gives me a good foot massage.

August 15

I wander through my own private wasteland, wondering if I will ever walk again. It seems such a small thing to want, so easy for most. Is it a realistic goal for me? Something in me is uncertain but determined. It takes time – I have the rest of my life. I get so tired of sitting. Maybe that in itself will be impetus enough to get me back on my feet.

Letter from Mary, visit from Susan, Debbie's mother Phyllis lights a candle for me, Richard rubs my back. Simple caring.

August 16

Richard's 39th birthday. One thing I am very good at and that is taking the scraps that other people give to me and making something out of it – be it crocheting scraps of wool into a blanket or scarf, or hearing a snatch of conversation that I can use to apply to my life. I treasure this ability. It has proven itself to be invaluable, time and time again. To be able to make something out of nothing is one of the secrets and privileges of my life.

Today has been one long party. Betty arrived about noon with fresh wild blueberries, tapes, a new red notebook. We spent the afternoon leisurely talking, winding wool, washing my hair. What a treat for me. Then Richard came with a new multi-colored blouse for me, a set of head phones, candy, magazines. I began to wonder whose birthday it was. He had also bought some shirts and records for himself, and Betty brought him some "toys" – a miniature bicycle and a cassette rack. Martha dropped in, and Ann and Mavis. A busy day.

Another birthday party tonight with Ted and Debbie and Richard – with all the trimmings. A chocolate cake baked by

Richard's mother, candles to blow out, wine, cards, and fresh-cut flowers for me. A nightgown from Edythe and George for me. What a day – I could have danced all night. Not at all tired. My strength and energy must be returning.

August 17

I have such a need to talk these days – and a need for physical contact. As I lose my eyesight my sense of touch becomes more and more important. My hearing too has been affected, i.e., diminished. For whatever reason I often have difficulty hearing or identifying where a sound is coming from. I hear people talking but sometimes don't know what they are saying. It must be that our senses are interrelated, perhaps even interdependent. We hear with our eyes, see with our ears, our fingertips. I am also losing sensation in the two middle fingers of my left hand.

So I reach out to make contact – verbal, tactile. I need to be able to feel the livingness of my own body and spirit and that of others – and all things. I need this reassurance that I exist, that I am important to someone, be it casual acquaintance or intimate friend.

Susan brings two more drawings from Samantha. Wonderful. I now have three of them stuck to the cupboard doors. Brandy dropped in for a chat. He's here from New York for a few days.

Franka (my favourite twenty year old nurse) brought me white earrings to go with my white necklace. They match perfectly. Franka was so excited at finding just the right ones. She kept hugging me as she is leaving this floor to work in the OR. Her Italian ancestors would have been proud. That innocent open demonstrative affection – I love it. So different from North American reticence. Her warmth and genuine affection satisfy my need for contact. I missed Richard being here tonight for that very reason. He usually rubs my foot or back and we hug a lot. I almost can't sleep at night without my hug. I always wrap my arms around my pillow as a substitute.

August 18

It is 9:45 a.m. and I am sitting here waiting for Richard to take me home for the day. I have a wheelchair to get around in. It's really easy to operate and reasonably comfortable. It's cool today after all this muggy weather we've had for the last few weeks.

It seems that one of the secrets of life is to be able to use the time we spend waiting constructively. In fact, the measure of a man depends on what he does with his life while waiting. Does he moan and groan about having to wait? Does he become impatient and annoyed? Does he daydream? Is it a time for reflection? Or making plans for the future? Or centering oneself? The possibilities are endless. Except sometimes (like today) I just get plain restless when I am looking forward to something and have to wait – and all my fine philosophical thoughts go out the window! A sense of humour helps and I realize that a great deal of the time, I'm full of shit with my lofty words and thoughts.

Had a great day at home. Denys (my hairdresser) came to the house and cut my hair very short. Richard made hamburgers and cooked corn that Rick O. brought from the market.

I fell asleep and dreamed that I had toes like claws growing out of my stump. Then there were thousands of claws in the air flying around attacking us. I screamed at Richard, "It won't work. You don't really want me here. It'll never work." I had a similar nightmare the last time I was home. It must be deep inside, this fear of the world outside the hospital.

August 19

Have been here for two months today. There is a woman next door who has had a stroke and is now aphasic (which means her speech is affected). She makes sounds that she thinks are words and says no when she means yes. She cries a lot, screams sometimes from frustration at not being able to communicate. It must be terrible. I don't think I could deal with that since communication and contact are so important to me. I have my tape recorder now with me here – will begin to use it for my thoughts, feelings, conversations too. It should be an adventure and a challenge – which I always look for to make my life more interesting. Creative tasks. Writing a lot these days. Both the ordinary events of daily life and the extraordinary inner journey I am on. They are so interrelated, sometimes I cannot distinguish between the two. My life is certainly unique and fascinating to me, as are the lives of everyone around me. Each person has something special to offer – and something special that they need. Isn't it wonderful that we all fit into each other's lives, that we can learn from others, that we can all teach each other. A miracle of existence.

Richard wheeled me down to the sunroom tonight where we watched the lightning and listened to the rolling thunder. So simple and satisfying.

August 20

Back in surgery tomorrow to clean up the stump. I feel very blue tonight, on the verge of depression. I wish my mother were here.

Called my parents and feel much better. It is difficult for me to reach out to them. I always play the "strong one" yet when I do reach out and say I need you they respond. It makes them feel good to know that they are important to me, that they can help me, that they make me feel better.

What disturbs me is transferring to the isolation floor after surgery. I hate the idea of being closed in, confined, just when I need contact the most.

August 21

Waiting for surgery. Another nightmare, surrounded by doctors doing things to my head and legs. Wake up sobbing as anesthetist tells me that they will use a spinal anesthetic. I sob so loudly and tell him I'm afraid I'll never walk again, that I'm afraid of the feeling of paralysis from the spinal. He changes his mind and says he'll give me a general. He gives me Valium to calm me down. I relax. Surgery is over and I feel terrific – no ill side effects that evening at all. Richard and Rick O. came over this evening and helped me "redecorate" my new room in isolation – "nesting," as Susan would call it. It's much smaller, so that everything is within reach. It also allows me a chance to get in touch with my solitude again. Rick bought the perfect book to read to me, by May Sarton, a poet who has written *Journal of a Solitude,* a wonderful, simple, honest reflection on life. She talks a great deal about the natural cycles of nature both organically and metaphorically. It compels and inspires me to write. If I could have the kind of insight she has at sixty I would be perfectly content. I don't mean content in terms of happiness – for life is difficult much of the time and meant to be that way so that we can grow in spirit. I mean content in terms of fullness, richness of experience. I want it all – the joy, the suffering, the loneliness, the intimacy, the knowledge of self and the other.

It is 2:30 a.m., I have slept two hours and am now awake and in pain. I drink ice water and eat licorice. My throat is sore from the tube they put into my lungs during surgery. The cool water soothes my throat and my fiery spirit. I have learned so much these last three years about myself, about others, about relationships, about taking time to look around me and see the miraculous. Before, I was too busy being involved, being identified with my ever-so-important tasks. Now I know that my relationships and my solitude are the most important.

4 a.m. Listening to Betty's "Water Music" that she brought on tape – guitar or harp and flute. Peaceful after a rocky day. Now a cello – sounds like Paul Horn on flute, a violin trembles, flute quavers, sound of water or gentle rain, perfect for my mood and the time of night. Oriental chimes in the wind or tinkling glass, delicate shades of night.

Since I am in isolation and have no idea of the outside world, I feel strangely secure, protected, inviolate. My Persian violet, African violet and carnations that Rick brought are all thriving and remind me that there is life outside. All I see through the window is blackness. Inside my cosy shell-like room there is music and light and flowing water washing over all, clearing my spirit, cleansing my soul. At this moment I am at peace.

If there is deep love involved, there is deep responsibility toward it.
(May Sarton)

August 22

Back in my isolation room after dialysis. Susan comes to see me and read from Carl Jung's *Memories, Dreams, Reflections*. I am sick to my stomach so we cut the reading short. Richard is in the country with Bill (Susan's husband). Graham and I have a long talk earlier today about uncertainty and change. We all look forward to a change in routine but at the same time are afraid of change and the uncertainty that goes with it. Change can be a challenge that one goes forth to meet – or it can be an escape that one shies away from with fear and trembling.

I miss my room on the 18th floor, my room with a view of the city lit up at night. I used to wake up almost every night around 2 or 3 a.m. and watch the city glow. Here, in isolation, I have only views of myself. I rediscover my solitude.

August 25

I am just coming out of a two-day slump, a reaction to the surgery and general stress, as always accompanied by vomiting and inability to eat. Today I am very tired but managed to type a letter to Mary and Bob. Graham dropped by this evening, almost as in answer to my silent cry for him to come last night and help me figure out why I was so distressed. I remember thinking as I bent over the kidney basin last night that the basin was full of my unexpressed anger (not anger at anyone but anger in general that all this is happening to me). I have nowhere to direct the anger so it turns inward and makes me sick to my stomach – and I defeat myself because I have no positive energy to help the healing process. I talk to Graham and tell him my thoughts. Now I can muster my forces to continue the battle, to help my body heal itself so that I can walk again. Richard comes in to see me this evening and fills me with added strength. My anger dissolves.

It is late at night, about 11 or so. There was a "99" (cardiac arrest) a few minutes ago, and all the nurses ran to help. It's very scary, that sound of the emergency buzzer and the urgent voice over the intercom, "99, 99, 99." It's just about the worst sound I've ever heard.

August 29

Getting in touch with myself has become a bizarre event. Dreams, nightmares, memories. I have stopped taking Demerol and morphine for pain and am "coming down" hard. At least I'm not throwing up any more. I can stand anything except nausea.

August 30

Wise words of Yogi Berra, "It ain't over till it's over." I feel like I'll never get out of here. Isolation has got to be the darkest, most depressing part of this journey. All I want to do is sleep. It's hard to motivate myself in the dark. Are my eyes getting worse or is it just dark in here? These days I am glad to go to dialysis – at least it's brighter than isolation. I've got to get better and get out of here, out of this state.

There was a wonderful thunderstorm yesterday that rolled over the city and cooled things off for a while. But we need another one today to clear the air (and my head). I lay here quite happily listen-

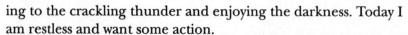

ing to the crackling thunder and enjoying the darkness. Today I am restless and want some action.

Another storm – at least it breaks the monotony. I wish I were outside in the middle of it. Perhaps a stroke of lightning would brighten me up. Dr. B. says the stump looks better than he expected. Hope?

August 31

Mother came for the day on Monday. She read me quotes that her mother had written in a book: it seems that this compulsion to write runs in the family. My mother and Patsy and my father. Mother read my father's recollections of his experiences here in the Royal Victoria Hospital. Fascinating account. Hospitals are strange places. One often gets into unusual states.

They have moved me across the hall to #24 tonight where there is more light so that I can see to continue with my quilt and crocheting. I feel better already. The light affects my spirit.

Long talk with George over the phone. We are still good friends – in many ways closer than ever. I think he has learned much about his own solitude, has come to feel less restless with himself, less full of need. I, on the other hand, have learned to be less independent, more able to reach out to give and receive, less isolated. We talk of harmony, balance, grace, laughter and perspective. We talk about the past, the present. We talk warmly and express affection without fear or demands. He says I will always be a part of his life, as he is a part of mine.

Night falls. I see the lights of the city through my window. They cheer me as time slowly passes.

There is no tomorrow. What about this afternoon?
(Line from the cover of a novel called *Dudley*, found lying in a washroom)

September 1

Have slept almost all morning. Can't understand why I am so tired. It is decidedly brighter in this room so I shall work on my quilt this afternoon and catch up with my neglected "work." I feel neglected myself today – haven't seen anyone since 8 a.m. It's lunch time.

I get very impatient with myself when I get into this complaining state. There should always be new beginnings. Perhaps complaining is merely an indication that it is time for a new beginning, a new cycle. I want so much to make, to create a useful life, not to waste these precious moments in useless anger and self-pity. I have every justification, every excuse for crying the blues and yet my life is wondrous and full of unique, uncommon opportunities. I watch healthy people and know that somewhere within me there is a spark of that health that keeps the healing force alive. I will never fully understand why my body has to go through all this when my spirit feels so healthy. Every life experience has something to teach us. I just wish this lesson were over so I can get on with my life. These "limbo" periods are sometimes interminable, though often illuminating in retrospect.

I think sometimes that I perhaps am supposed to be an inspiration to others. Is that my real purpose? It embarrasses me oftentimes when I feel so uninspiring and I feel the expectations in other's eyes. I am so ordinary most of the time. Maybe inspiration itself is very ordinary, coming unexpectedly in the midst of everyday life. We are all so greedy for the extraordinary that perhaps we miss what is right in front of us. It is a question of learning how to see, how to look and "where to look among the garbage and the flowers" (Leonard Cohen, "Suzanne").

My friend Rick always brings a lively bouquet of flowers fresh from the Jean Talon Market along with a bagful of apples and corn for Richard. He has been most attentive and kind – he redecorates my wall with cards and finds two miniature cacti to fit in a couple of rooster-painted eggcups. He reads to me, we laugh, we gossip, we talk of loneliness and boredom. He says there must be some way to get through the emptiness after a relationship is over. I think the only way through it is through it. There doesn't seem to be any way to avoid emptiness and pain but to let it come – and let it go.

September 2

I am vaguely aware that others may read this journal. It changes the writing somewhat, and I wonder if I try unconsciously to present myself in a little less than honest light – if I try to make myself sound more "presentable." Perhaps we are always doing that, and to some extent it is probably a good thing that we make the effort to be more than we are.

It is interesting to trace one's life back to the early days and discover how one acted as a child to get attention. Some of us did it by "being good," others by throwing temper tantrums, others by being cute or performing or demanding or fighting or ... One of my primary ways of getting attention, getting what I wanted, was by getting sick. And because it worked very well, I did it frequently and learned that everyone gave me whatever I wanted when I was ill (mostly with minor ailments like colds). I was a "delicate" child. Trouble is that I learned too well and now am stuck with my childhood device. I often wonder how far I have to go to get the attention I need. I am trying to learn new, less destructive ways to amuse and "entertain," to listen and be more sensitive to the needs of others. Interesting how we carry those seeds planted in childhood into our adult life, long past the age when they are necessary for our survival. We learn early how to get those around us to respond to our needs. Then we continue to use those mechanisms as they become firmly entrenched habits. It would seem, then, that we should be very careful when responding to the needs of others – our response may only encourage an unpleasant and unnecessary childhood habit.

When I look back I remember that I was a somewhat secretive child and until recently had such difficulty identifying my needs to the point of excruciating frustration. I have learned through the years to recognize my needs and am better able to express them and consequently find solutions. I wonder why I still need to get sick.

I understand that there are physical as well as emotional reasons for my illness. Not all of my ailments are an attention-getting device!

Another dream as I fall asleep. I am the dreamer and the dream. I am the child and I am the mother. There is a large black car. I cannot get the brakes to hold. The child is in front of the car and I cannot keep it from running over the child. It is winter. Everywhere there is snow and woods. The car runs over the child and she crawls up through the front of the car to the inside (reverse birth process if car is womb). I am outside the car. it seems I keep trying to rescue this child. The car keeps trying to run it down. What is the meaning? That I must destroy myself so that I can be reborn? The child is clever and seems able to survive on its own. First dream I remember having in which I am both mother and child. I am the dreamer and the dream. The gypsy stands naked at my back door and beckons me to follow. A wolf howls across the icy landscape and crystal tears fall in mourning for the fading light. Must I give up so much to achieve so little? Out of the cradle endlessly rocking. I think this is a quote from somewhere. I know not from whence it comes but I like it.

September 3

Fall is in the air on this Labour Day. The summer has passed me by. I have experienced it only through clouded windows with an occasional breath of fresh air.

The light is strangely diffuse and monotonous – flat with few highlights but many shadows. My wall is covered with colourful cards and posters that cheer me yet seem unreal – places I will never see, longing imaginations, memories, dreams. Fresh flowers and cacti adorn my window ledge. A few gourds that foretell of autumn.

Corn Cheese Casserole
(Marion Faith)

1 1/2 c. corn	1 Tbsp. melted butter
1 c. crackers	2 c. scalded milk
1 1/2 c. grated cheese	2 eggs

Combine all ingredients except eggs and milk.
Beat egg yolks and add to warm milk. Add to other ingredients.
Fold in stiffly beaten egg whites.
Put into greased casserole and bake 40 minutes at 350°.

September 4

Betty and Bob (twenty-three) here for a couple of hours on their way to Ottawa where Bob goes to Carleton University (Sociology). We talk of attitudes and choices, power and politics.

I watch a program on PBS about Vietnam and I think how privileged we are and how blasé we are about our comfortable lives. We may have our complaints great and small, but we do not spend every night wondering where the next bomb will fall or whether we will wake up in the morning. We take our lives so much for granted that when the least little thing doesn't go as we expect, we rant and rave and talk about our rights. How pompous we all are sometimes.

I'm not suggesting that we should all become beggars and swear vows of poverty and pray with religious fervour ... only perhaps we should remember that we do live in the most privileged

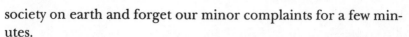

society on earth and forget our minor complaints for a few minutes.

My friend Joan calls and says her apartment was burglarized while she was away in Newfoundland. All the treasures given to her by her adopted family are gone. Irreplaceable things that are of no value to anyone else. I felt so sorry for her – not only does she not know her parentage, she no longer has any of the trinkets and treasures given to her by the family and friends who gave her her childhood. I wanted to make things right for her and felt so helpless when I realized there was nothing I could do.

September 5

Plastic surgeons here this morning. They may have to do a skin graft to cover the wound, which means I may be here for a good while yet. Fortunately I have lots of projects – scarves and scrapbooks, stories to write, a quilt to finish and a sweater that I started six years ago. Even a wall hanging if I get desperate – and always the journal that I use to record my daily existence and the occasional illumination. I have a lot of pages to fill, and few thoughts. However, every day brings something new.

Rick reads to me from Theodore Dreiser, Margaret Atwood and May Sarton. Such varied sensibilities. Atwood with her crisp, hard-edged disdain; Sarton the romantic, poetic, more luxuriant and sensual; Dreiser literary and graphically descriptive with astute, accurate powers of observation. An inventory of an age. I like these soirées.

In keeping with Dreiser and his turn-of-the-century portraits, I watch a PBS program about the labour movement in the early 1900's up to the depression. Long lines of men on "relief row"; laments and mournful ballads of miners and sharecroppers, tearful tunes of hardship and hope sung by Woody Guthrie, Big Bill Broonsy, Sonny Terry and Brownie McGee. No embellishment here, or extravagant laser-light spectacles – just simple men and women with their straightforward, honest and unadorned phrases.

A preacher whips the crowd into religious fever and cools their spirit by full-body baptism. Sweet harmonies, snow-covered graves, mountain mornings, white-hooded klansmen, black and white in opposition, darkened faces from the mines where there are no differences and everyone is just a worker – a pair of hands, a bent back. Hunger and toil, yet always great belief in tomorrow and the future of America. "I looked at the sun, and the sun looked high."

Liberty, independence, freedom, equal rights, security – have we progressed at all? Is the quality of life any better? Do we fight just for survival? We are told that Social Security will solve the ills of the world; or religion or alcohol will. And on and on – always a belief in some system or institution or ideology or new purchase. Always something *other*. We do not like to accept the responsibility for our own lives. We take the credit when everything goes well, but try to find someone or something else when our lives don't work. I am not exempt from this. I have my list of "blameables."

We of the "baby boom" (war and post-war) have been fortunate in this country and have never really had to test our survival skills or refine them due to a national or international disaster – no world war, no real economic crisis, etc. We are largely the children of imagined hardship. We are allowed to choose our form of suffering – hence neurosis, indebtedness, marital crises, drug dependence, illness and other products of affluence and boredom. It is so easy for me to criticize, living as I do: well-protected, comfortably buffered against most of the terrors and trials. I criticize mostly my own attitudes, my lack of any real contribution to society. I am both lazy and generous within a small circle. I have both paid my debt and find myself owing my very life to so many who have provided a support system. I am indulgent and frivolous, severe and undisciplined and can justify it all. I even fool myself, and if asked to show my cards, often pull out the ace up my sleeve.

I guess we're all going to be what we're going to be.
(line from a Don Williams song)

September 6

Sun pours in my window. The plants Betty brought from the wild and Rick's cacti and Mother Owen's African violet greet the dawn. I have difficulty with clichés but I do love the cheery bright reflections, the irregular patterns of light and shadow that fall across my bed.

I ought to spend more time trying to refine my words but the urgency to communicate, to catch the moment before it fades to memory, precludes deliberation. Writing is such a fickle occupation. It eludes me often – it seems too slow for my flighty mind. Other times I can labour for hours to find one word, one phrase to sculpt it, or the exact nuance that rings true and sparkles with honesty and clarity. There is nothing quite like the feeling of having written a well-crafted phrase, like a beautiful piece of pottery or a painting. Even a lucid conversation can delight my senses, as well as challenge my mind.

It seems that we only create what we are, that our creations are extensions of what we have become or projections of where we would like to go with our inner selves. Is it really possible to create a dishonest piece of work? I wonder – we probably betray ourselves, in the sense of giving ourselves away, with our creations. I look at the scarf I have just finished crocheting and see the unevenness, the not-so-carefully-hidden loose ends, the brightness of reds, orange, royal blue, yellow, purple, the disregard for uniformity, for perfection, the "hand-made" quality of it all. I rather like the flaws; they please me. The scarf, like my self, is unfinished. It will be given away to whoever likes it. It was not made for anyone in particular but because of my own need to make something, to do something with these long stretches of time as I wait for my wound to heal.

I am getting to appreciate this time I have. It is getting so I hate to be interrupted for dialysis, dressing changes, doctor's visits.

Autumn approaches, always for me a time of new beginnings – probably that feeling goes back to my school days and the excitement I felt about going back to school. It was another way that I received positive attention from my elders because I always did well. But also autumn leads me toward my true self, the time for reflection and memory, the time to take stock and gather my strength after the dissipation of summer.

Autumn renews my spirit – the crisp air that crackles outside my window, the slowly darkening sky that preludes winter, the days that grow more precious as they grow shorter, the sun that slants lower each day on the horizon, the leaves that fall leaving barren the branches, the sweaters and jackets that suddenly are necessary to ward off the chill. Autumn is for remembrance of other autumns, other beginnings. Most of all it is a time of transition.

Welsh Rarebit
2 c. sharp cheese   paprika
1/2 c. beer, milk or tomato soup
Melt over hot water. Pour over toast or English muffin.

Fruit Salad
canned fruit salad, pineapple, mandarins, etc.
1 pkg. lemon pudding mix
coconut

Banana Delight
Cut wedge shape lengthwise out of banana (leave peel on). Fill with chocolate chips and marshmallow. Fold peel over and wrap banana in tin foil. Heat in oven or toss in hot coals to melt chocolate and marshmallow. (You have to see this to believe it.) ... Sounds terrific.

September 7
Sun streams into my small space and fills in the shadowy corners. Summer returns briefly. It is so bright that my eyes water as I try to catch a few rays on my face. I wake at 7 a.m. and have an hour of silence before breakfast. I am impatient because my stomach growls for oatmeal and cream. The man with the mop freshens the floor with his pine-scented mop – it smells very antiseptic, quite pleasant really – yet I long for the real smell of the woods. Betty brought bunchberries and some other foliage with pink and blue berries the other day.

I feel the chill somewhere inside myself although my skin is warm to the touch. My moods swing randomly, with abandon, with no discernible sense. I am up, I am down, I am dull, I am euphoric, I am brittle and sensitive, tough and inviolate. As the seasons change, so do I follow their cycle. I ought to be accustomed to the fluctuations by now. But still there are surprises as I travel through the highs and lows.

I waste lots of time making plans about all the things I am going to do. I have lots of ideas for projects that never get started or that I never finish even if I do manage to muster the energy to start.

September 8
Old photographs – my project for the day. They speak of another era long before I was born – my family history. I look at photos of my mother and father when they were young and I wonder who they were, what they felt and thought about, their experiences, their relationship. Was it so different from mine? I look very much like my mother when she was my age. She looks happy and well

cared for, protected from the harsher realities of life, although I don't suppose any of us reaches the age of forty without a few burdens to shoulder.

Photographs – what do they reveal? We always try to look our best when being photographed. I wonder how much we can conceal? Or in the very act of trying to do so, do we betray our true nature? Interesting to look at old photos to see who stands beside whom, who smiles, who frowns, who is relaxed, who is stiff and who is always missing from the family group. They can tell us a lot about family relationships.

"Language creates social reality." (From a program of PBS on language.) Is it true then that our attitudes are shaped by the words we speak? For instance, are we more likely to have a positive outlook if the words we use are positive?

Wonderful letter from Aunt Mary. Richard read it to me. She tells tales of her family life simply, honestly, modestly. I love to hear stories of days gone by. My mother and father are both very good at it, as are many older people. What treasures are stored in people's minds.

Some days I have so little to write about – or I cannot follow a single thought for long or see the relatedness of things. What has happened today? Ann dropped in – we talk of "feminine consciousness," a term we both abhor, especially when the emphasis is placed on the (so-called) disadvantages of being female. What disturbs me most of all is women who feel they must compete with men to be equal while they lose the one advantage they really have – that of being female! Personally, I like being a woman.

Martha came in and washed my very dirty white sweater. Just like having a real sister. We talk about acupuncture and mutual friends, eat egg sandwiches and Peak Frean garden cremes. I show her photos of our wedding. I have been working on my photo album all day – sorting, arranging and musing, remembering.

I talk to Richard on the phone – he is crying, thinking about his father singing in the morning, Mary's letter. I said, "This is your lovely wife speaking," and he burst into tears. He is letting his feelings show more and more now. I love him for that. He visits me later and we spend an hour quietly together. He rubs my back and foot.

Rick called and said he would be over tomorrow after 1 p.m. and we could read the *New York Sunday Times* together. We also need to re-do the wall. He says he is absorbed in his solitude today. I called Joan to see if she would help me with some research. She has a toothache and her kitchen ceiling fell down last night. She feels miserable. I don't wonder.

Well, I think I've finally run out of words. This is like writing a letter to a friend, a very non-critical friend. Am I wasting time with this journal or would I be just as well off writing letters?

September 9

My right hand is numb this morning. I hope it is only temporary – that I slept on it the wrong way. I hate this lack of sensation; it has been there in my left hand for over a month. What next do I have to endure?

Sunday morning preachers' special; it bores me and appalls me to see so many of the faithful listening to this revivalist advertising heavenly virtues like a box of Tide. The sinners pray to be saved and delivered from the devil. Can they believe this form of religiosity? For me, religion has never been a market-place item to be displayed ostentatiously, but a private, personal experience between the individual and whatever power he believes in. No public reverence, no mass ministry, no TV oratory. Walk in the name of Jesus. All this interspersed with ads for latex paint and mail fraud and morning stretch. Inspiring messages that dull the spirit and turn us into a nation of sheep.

Enough of this. Tirades are tiresome, especially on such a gloriously sunny day. I am a pagan as I worship the sun and the cool air, flowers that bloom on my windowsill, cacti that survive with little water, my colourful posters and cards. I give thanks for all the generous people who have helped me, cheered me, sat with me. I am grateful for my parents, my husband, my friends, my nurses and doctors who care for me and who wish me well.

This is my religion. My faith is in humanness, in the miracles that come through the generosity of others. There is a power greater than all of us, there is a mystery and a design to the universe that makes our lives extraordinary.

A very heart-wrenching man on the program I have just finished criticizing says, "Blessed are they who have dreams and are willing to pay the price to make them come true." He was born without legs and now runs a school for 240 "handicapped" children. A man who knows that to be "disadvantaged" is really a rare privilege – that it provides a special kind of challenge and triumph. Whether it be faith in God or faith in oneself – or both – is irrelevant. As long as one goes forward with humility, acknowledging the generosity of life and the life-givers, there can be no self-pity, hostility or recriminations. We so often forget to appreciate the wonder.

I'm drooling over the *New York Times Fashion Magazine.* I can hardly wait to wear my clothes again. It has been so long since I've been dressed. If I had money I'd spend it all on clothes, lingerie and jewelry. Perfume, too. Ah, the luxury of being female. Furs don't interest me too much but I am very conscious of texture. I love silk and drapey fabrics, but also wool and tweeds. I love warm colours – reds and orange and yellows. Not too crazy about pastels. I also like the neutral shades – gray and white and black with a splash of Chinese red or yellow. My mother likes me to wear blue because it brings out my eyes. I like to wear colours I can see. Black, navy, brown, dark green all look the same to me; I have difficulty distinguishing them. I also have trouble with white, yellow and pink. The only colour I can really be sure of is red.

The Pope has arrived in Quebec City and will be in Montreal on Tuesday. The whole city is on its knees. There is to be a mass in Jarry Park and a youth rally at Olympic Stadium. Roads are being blocked off, security is tight, the Popemobile is bulletproof, and armed guards are everywhere. A lot of nervous officials stand by, especially since last Monday's Labour Day bombing in Central Station in which three people were killed and many more injured. We are beginning to be a nation of violent people – or rather, there are more frequent outbursts of violence, political and senseless. What does it prove or improve?

John called from the ballpark. He and Debbie are trying to work things out with the aid of group counseling. The statistics say that one in four marriages break up. What is happening to the family? The individual and his/her relationships? The responsibility lies with us all. It seems that often one's life is just a matter of sheer luck to choose the right mate or at least someone with whom it is possible to communicate. We are such complex mixtures of needs and desires, hopes, dreams, talents, inadequacies. It is rare to find the perfect match and we all expect so much from others, as well as demanding a great deal from ourselves. Relax and enjoy what is there rather than complain about what is lacking.... Good advice that I don't always adhere to.

Elizabeth calls from Vancouver after a talk with our mutual friend Paul. I haven't heard from her for years. We shared a house on St. Laurent before I moved in with Richard in '75. She sounds the same; still that wonderful merry laugh.

Rick reads to me from the *New York Times* about John Cheever, my favourite writer, alcoholic, attracted to both men and women, genius with a pen, renegade like so other many luminaries. The article is written by his daughter Susan Cheever, also a writer and brilliant in her own way. We also read about Antonia Fraser, a prolific historian and mystery writer. I have never read her books but she sounds fascinating. Aunt Mary has mentioned her and her *Mary, Queen of Scots*. I have sent May Sarton's *Journal of a Solitude* to Mary for her comments.

Rick brings cattails and daisies and fixes up my wall. At least I have a new arrangement to look at. It is much more pleasing to my withering eyesight. I am very aware of pattern, design, shape and balance between the light and the dark. Now the wall is better proportioned, more colourful, less ranging and scattered.

Richard comes early tonight as he is going to a concert later in the evening. We watch tennis finals – the US Open with McEnroe and Lendl. Later I watch a show about Marco Polo and his travels in the East. Man has always been on a search for himself and other unconquered lands. That quest has always been unquenchable and can either form the root of his deepest dissatisfaction or the pinnacle of his greatest delight. It is, at least in part, what keeps him alive and motivates his spirit. The quest, the fascination with the unknown, with adventure, with the pursuit of his dreams.

I wake at 3:30 a.m., in pain and shivering. What is it that will not let me sleep? I am disturbed by dreams and by the full moon, which always affects me. It is often the light that illuminates the pre-dawn sky. Tonight it is something else that prevents my slumber and causes me pain, some unsolved, arcane mystery hidden from consciousness. Perhaps it is the trepidation I feel about more surgery, skin graft and a further period of healing – the uncertainty and anticipation of a new set of circumstances, a new pain. Imagination is always far worse than the event itself. I am wide awake now and know I will be tired in the morning. I like the mornings very much and seem to need the light to get started on anything. Perhaps I ate too many cookies before retiring and my digestive juices are protesting. What else could it be?

My parents may come to see me near the end of the week and that is always cause for both joy and concern, especially with my father's broken hip. I hope they manage it without too much trouble for I dearly love to see them both but only if they are in good spirits. I am so easily affected by another's mood, fragile and brittle like glass. I am no good at all under tension.

My compulsion to write occupies the long days, perhaps put to better use. I have stopped crocheting and quilting for the moment, afraid that I am not doing a very respectable job due to eyesight, but that is no excuse. It's just easier not to do it, to be lazy and procrastinate. Writing stories and letters, too, requires an extra effort these days.

I need someone to work with. In that respect I am like my father, who always liked to have someone around with whom he could discuss things. I remember spending hours with him composing letters and talking. I always hated it at the time, these discussions. Now I understand what that was really all about. I got to know him very well during those sessions.

The pain has subsided somewhat after a shot of Demerol. Amazing drug. In fact I don't really know how it works, except that it takes away the pain both physically and mentally and relaxes my torment. I will try to sleep again. I have a sense of urgency these days, as if my time is running out.

Perhaps, after all, true spirituality is only the ability to respond to the moment, with no preconceptions, expectations or associations.
(K.T.B.)

September 10

Still in pain this morning after a restless night. The surgeons are supposed to look at my stump this week and assess the situation – whether it needs a skin graft or just close the wound. Another painful stretch ahead.

Richard opens my window so I can catch a whiff of fresh air after an all-day drizzle. Being in isolation, we're not supposed to open the window because of germs and dust from outside. But I can't stand the stuffiness in here. The air is so stale and unhealthy. Even my flowers and plants like the freshness.

The Pope is supposed to pass by the hospital tomorrow morning between 7:30 and 8. He is really causing quite a stir all over

Quebec among the devout and cynics alike. I am not one of the devout and have to watch what I say and to whom. My comments tend to be offensive and slightly sarcastic. But then, I have no grounds for criticizing others for their beliefs. Richard is going to the mass in Jarry Park tomorrow with Bill. It should be quite an event.

Richard brings his friend Paul to see me tonight. He is an interesting young man of twenty-five, one of the few who hasn't reached the age of disillusionment. He still has that sense of wonder about the universe. Interested in the current contemporary scene, a musician with a load of talent, ambitious, opinionated (sometimes obnoxiously so), some kind of rift between him and his father. He has just received a letter from him after a couple of years. He says there are three questions that a parent has about his child: Are you alive? How are you? What are you doing? Paul can be tiresome when he starts his talk, impressed by the last thing he has read or the last person he's talked to, when he sounds as if his truth is the only possibility. Easy to anger but usually polite and amusing. I wrote a story for him about him as a child, a kite, his grandmother, his father – things and incidents he related, a bit of fiction and imaginary conversation.

I am dopey tonight from a shot of Gravol. I can hardly keep my eyes open or write in a straight line. I should go to bed but obstinately sit up to watch "The National" on CBC. I cannot find a comfortable sleeping position so I stay awake even after sleeping pills and the like. I sleep sporadically, a couple of hours at a time. It seems there is something on my mind. In my dreams I bang my stump and learn to hop around on one leg. I still have a great deal of phantom sensation which keeps me awake and uncomfortable. The window is closed now and even though it is much quieter, it is also stuffy and claustrophobic.

He's a walking contradiction, partly truth and partly fiction.
(Kris Kristofferson)

September 11

I have been watching the televised broadcast of the Pope in Montreal. It has affected me strangely. Despite the pomp and fuss, there is something genuine about this man, a kind of energy that is exuded by his presence. There is something that happens when a large group of people are together all concentrating on the same thing – a ripple of energy of a special nature that elevates each individual beyond what he himself could obtain on his own. I remember years ago in New York City going to see Katharine Kuhlman, a well-known faith healer. As she walked onto the stage in the ballroom of the Americana Hotel amidst a crowd of thousands of hopeful people, there was a hush and a flood of warmth that swept over the crowd waiting expectantly. With that energy available, some very unusual things happen; miracles do take place. I found that the tears were pouring down my cheeks. Today the Pope celebrates mass. I see people reach out their hands to touch his outstretched hand. I wish I could have touched his hand.

Watching the Pope with a large group of children is a rare treat. He beams as children reach out for a glance, a kiss, a pat on the head. They crowd around almost blocking his path but it is obvious that he and they love it. He is truly in his element when close to the people, not so good when making speeches. They all join hands together and repeat the Lord's Prayer. They chant "Vive le Pape." One kid grabs his head and removes his cap. Many children hold out paper rosaries, notes of greeting, gifts handmade and loving; a caring tribute to a gentle man. He tells them that they each have a contribution to make, a gift to give. He makes each child feel important. Bunches of balloons rise outside in Place d'Armes in front of Notre Dame Basilica. Each has a message inside for anyone who finds one. The CBC announcer calls it wonderful emotional chaos.

Later the youth rally at the Olympic Stadium. A dance of fear and shadows, the triumph of faith and light. John Paul II is given a pair of doves in a cage as a symbolic gesture of peace. He lifts the cage over the doves; they do not fly away. A great man. He and the two teenagers who presented the doves ruffle the doves' feathers and smooth them out again. The crowd cheers. Richard cries and tells me how much he loves me.

This visit from the Pope has imbued us all with new energy of a very special nature. My scepticism is still rampant but I do feel that I have at least been brushed by a great presence. His speech to the young people tonight was the most accessible yet. He talked of love and confusion, shadow and light, of banishing the darkness by letting the light shine through. It is we who cast the shadows. We must get out of our own way. If each of us could let his little light shine, it would form a larger light by which we all could see better.

My father is coming on Saturday to see me. I have a feeling he is coming alone without mother. He called earlier today and didn't mention her at all. He is determined to come despite his broken hip. I don't think he realizes how much walking there is inside the hospital.

My eyes are still so heavy with sleep that I can hardly write, yet I must. What is this compulsion I have to record my feelings and thoughts? Are they so important? It's not so much what I say but that I must say it. A verbal portrait of life by a forty-one year old woman. I am old-fashioned and hold old-fashioned ideas. I still believe in marriage and raising children, although the latter seems remote for me. I think it is the greatest emptiness I will ever feel. I wonder what kind of parents Richard and I would have made. Probably not much different than others. It is certain that our relationship would have changed. This time away from each other has been good for both of us in terms of appreciating each other and taking each other for granted.

I am so very tired. My resistance is low and I feel a lack of strength physically, emotionally, morally, intellectually, spiritually. A kind of spiritual wasteland that does not point the direction to follow. I climb over rocks and venture through the woods and water. In my dreams there are many hazards; rocks that swallow people up, creatures that surface from the deep, mosses that entangle, threatening vegetation. There are others with me, sometimes as guides, sometimes to mislead. We never seem to reach our destination. Pilgrims in the wilderness, believers in tomorrow, today's passengers through this universe.

We are only guests here for a brief span, each leaving a footprint in the sand that is there for a while, then washed away by the tide, smooth and pristine as if we had never been here at all. A delicate impression. This journal is my footprint, my record of having been here, of having existed.

Since we have no heirs to remember us, I feel compelled to leave something of myself behind. Again I feel that time is short. I feel I am being stalked by I know not what. It is 3:30 a.m. now and I must go to bed before I pass out. I feel my life is a rich tapestry of separate strands that eventually will form a pattern that one can only see if I stand apart from it. That is also what this journal is all about – perspective and distance and the span in between. It is the movement back and forth between being intimately involved and calmly detached that illuminates the manuscript and gives it life.

Wisdom is no use without kindness.
(Don Juan, in *The Fire From Within*)

September 12

The morning sun lifts my spirits always. Glorious. I can't help feeling blessed. If I have felt abandoned in the past I don't mind it in the morning light.

I come back from dialysis and my room is dark. I turn on the light. it is only 2:30 in the afternoon. My psychiatrist, Graham, and I have an argument about the Pope, about light and dark, about religious politics and extravagance, about ostentatious ceremonial pomp. I argue that all that is irrelevant – look beneath the surface and find that many people have been touched by his visit. "Whatever gets you through the night is all right." I only believe that others have a right to their beliefs (even Graham!) and I have a right to mine.

I listen to Matthew reading *The Fire From Within* on tape. It is Carlos Casteneda's most recent book. Don Juan, the sorcerer, talks to Carlos about self-importance being the main obstacle to growth. He says when a man loses his self-importance he is invincible. As long as we have it, our egos can be easily bruised, even shattered.

My nurse, Sue, says she envies me because I have been forced to slow down and have the time to develop my talents like writing. She wants to write children's stories. I give her *Dragonkurd*. Yes, I do have time. I have also sacrificed a great deal. I've paid for that time. No regrets, but I would like to be able to walk around again.

"Toxic brain syndrome"; is that for real? It sounds ridiculous but is apparently quite serious. It just struck me as amusing. I feel that way sometimes.

Had a visit from a wonderful seventy-five year old volunteer. She came in and introduced herself and I, being slightly bored, asked her to sit down. We talked and she told me her life's experiences – about picking strawberries behind their house in "the old days." And about going to meet her father who worked for the Canadian Pacific Railroad and walked home along the tracks, which always make her nervous since he didn't hear well and she was afraid he would not hear an oncoming train. She told me about strawberry, rhubarb and her mother's plum jam. She talked about her husband, her arthritis as a teenager and the gold cure that eliminated it.

When she had finished, she suddenly looked up and laughed and said, "I've been a volunteer on this 5th floor for twelve years and I've never told anyone my life story. If I told my friends, they'd be bored stiff. But you just sat there looking so interested – I guess I got carried away." What a sweet lady she was. Made me feel good. I hope I made her feel good, too. She visits every Wednesday. Maybe I'll get the tape recorder out next time. A wonderful oral history is there.As she left she said, "May the sun continue to shine on you."

And on you, Mrs. S.

I talk to one of the nurses, Marie, after being sick to my stomach around 6 a.m. We talk about faith and optimism, about the Pope's visit, about prejudice and negative attitudes. In some small way, we have all been touched by his presence. I think it was an important event that has been very meaningful to many, particularly those capable of being open to it. It's fine if one doesn't believe in the tenets of the Catholic church as long as one does not close off completely to any and all forms of faith. One has to believe in something.

Admittedly, some things are more illuminating than others. But essentially all teachings have some divine truth to them despite their outward manifestations. We have lost so much of the original that often only the structure is left, the shell which both protects and limits the original light.

> *Power is in the hands of the one who holds the light.*
> (Jean-Claude, friend)

September 13

The head nurse, Nancy, tells me the parable of the light. There was once a beautiful light. People came from all around to worship and gain strength. Because the light was so precious and fragile, the people surrounded it with jewels and a great temple. Soon the light moved away from its original simple space, but the people still came and lit candles even though the true light had vanished. So too with many religions.

Cloudy day – and I have no ambition today after a wakeful night. Time to make a super effort, so I work on my scrapbook all morning, read the headlines, watch the Pope in New Brunswick on TV. If I can get started on something in the morning, I seem to have a better day – back to my old feelings of accomplishing something each day. it is important to me and I am learning to structure my time a little more profitably.

I always think I have so little to write about yet I have managed a thousand words or more every day. Not all of it is important or even very interesting, but it is a wonderful discipline and outlet for my energy. Since I don't move around a lot and am not really sick any more, it is necessary to find a channel for my excess energy. Writing helps me to focus while I am doing it and to be more observant when I am not. Now that I have made the super effort and denied my desire to sleep in, I find that I have more energy than I did earlier.

I have letters to write, another story for Samantha to work on and always the quilt and scarves to finish. I ought to complete one project before tackling another but I seem to function better when I have several projects on the go. I can't seem to do any one thing for very long; I thrive on variety and choice.

This journal records the mundane and the arcane: one has to look carefully to find the occasional gem. On the other hand, there is always something interesting along the path of daily existence. One cannot always be looking for precious stones when a plain ordinary rock series is better. It is more comfortable to sit on a rock to rest than to sit on a precious stone. Each has its role to play – "a time to every purpose under heaven."

Susan dropped by for an hour or so. I've almost finished the scarf made from the wool she gave me, so I will give it back to her transformed into a multi-coloured scarf. I have always been fascinated by transformations, the moment of transition from one state to another, that breathless hesitation before the breaking of a wave, the wonder-filled pause between the lightning and the thunder, the magnificent glow of a rising or setting sun. Transitions all. It is mysterious – an alchemist's universe that we live in.

Richard is starting to take singing lessons next week. Susan is planning to open a delicatessen in Huntingdon. She has a partner and it sounds good. Martha has started bar school and Joan is back working on her master's. Everyone is starting new projects. A sure sign of fall. it feels like there is a lot of energy available these days. Fall has always been my best season, my favourite time of year, when I seem to accomplish more than at any other time of year. It has a lot to do with a crispness in the air, an inhalation and exhalation that suddenly becomes smooth and regular like a strong heartbeat. The rhythms of nature seem to mirror my own natural rhythms. I am a fall person through and through.

September 14

The Pope continues on his journey. I continue on mine. Sometimes I feel it is a narrow pathway strung like a tightrope between opposing poles. Sometimes it is a broad highway, and comrades travel with me. The tightrope I walk alone, with uncertain balance.

Sometimes the pathway leads through sunlit meadows, pleasant and filled with fragrant grasses and subtle, delicate wildflowers. Sometimes the path leads through a darkened forest, dangerously full of traps and unfriendly beasts. Mostly the rough terrain. Sometimes I have to wait, chilled to the bone, surrounded by darkness, for someone to kindle a small fire that I might draw from it a little warmth and light. But I eventually find the path is clear for a time.

Don Juan talks about needing a petty tyrant in one's life to destroy self-importance. He says you are lucky to have such a person in your life. If not, then you have to go out and look for one. Such a tyrant helps to develop control, discipline, forbearance. But in order not to crumble and succumb to the petty tyrant's ploys, one must have a strategy to deal with him.

There are always people in everyone's life who "push our buttons" and to whom we respond with seething rage. It is our self-importance that gives them that power over us, causes us to lose our centre. As long as we are "on our edges," we can be easily defeated and crushed. I see where the petty tyrant could be of service, could show us to ourselves, could help to destroy our false pride, our strutting egomania. The thing is to be clever about our relationship to such a person and use the situation for our own purposes.

Martha is having a hard time with her mother and members of her family who tease her and treat her, as they always have, as if she were irrational and stupid. (Ironic that she is studying law.)

Anyway, they are her petty tyrants. She decided not to respond the way she habitually does with anger and hurt and caustic remarks. When she just ignored them, they stopped treating her badly. They have lost their power over her, and the relationship is better.

Had a transfusion today – two units of blood, as my hematocrit had dropped to thirteen. It is supposed to be over twenty. So I should feel energetic this weekend. Anemia is one of the annoyances of kidney failure that leaves me exhausted.

September 15

7 a.m. I awake early and cannot get back to sleep, so I turn on the TV and I write. It is freezing this morning. Overcast so far. I wait for the warming sunshine as I remember getting up at this hour to go to work in the bookstore so long ago. Thank God I don't have to do that anymore.

My eyesight is bothering me lately – obscurely clouded, which makes it difficult to do much. It's a worry. My vision is so precious to me. I hope I can keep it a bit longer. I fear all the changes in lifestyle if I don't. There are so many things I do not want to give up, like seeing a flower in bloom, stars and clouds overhead, trees bending in the wind, the faces of those I love, even colours and shapes. I look at everything carefully these days so that I may remember.

I get angry at all my infirmities, my limitations, and wonder what I could have accomplished if I were healthy and could see better. I hear the words courageous and brave and it causes me to suffer, as I have so little choice. I could give up, but it is in my nature to survive in any way I can invent.

Dreary thoughts for a dreary day.

Maybe a bath in the tub will help. I have learned all kinds of simple little tricks, like baths, to lift my spirits. It is important to do the things I can do easily at the moments when I feel so precariously balanced, to resume some sort of equilibrium.

Have finally finished the fringe on the multi-coloured scarf for Susan. Richard decided that it was too loud for him. He likes another one that I started with autumn colours of rust and brown, orange and green, yellow and amber.

My parents spend most of the afternoon with me. I laugh at myself as I realize they are disrupting my well-ordered little universe with their clutter, bags and briefcases, coats, hats, shoes and chatter. I love them both dearly but they do spread chaos wherever they go, leaving me breathless and worn out in their wake. Both of them have fallen asleep in the lounge, so I have a few moments to myself to recuperate. Being with them is like being entertained by a vaudeville act.

Richard came in for a few minutes on his way to play in the Metro. He sings "I Left My Heart in San Francisco" for my parents. They are impressed by his persistence and discipline. He sounds good today – is getting more confidence "performing," playing for other people. I'm happy for him.

I eat too much for supper – reflections of anxiety, impatience and relief that I am alone once more. I watch the continuing saga of the Pope in Canada. With the TV I have the privilege of being able to change channels or turn it off at will. I find it difficult being with anyone for more than two hours and sigh with great relief when I am finally alone. Blissful silence. Welcome solitude.

I am very tired tonight, having been awake since 6:30 a.m. It is now 11:30 p.m. and the nurses are changing shifts. My eyes are so heavy that I am falling asleep in the middle of a word. I want to write but I am just too tired. Already my writing is erratic.

I have lived in this world just long enough to look carefully the second time into things I am the most certain of the first time.
(Josh Billings)

September 16

I have slept all morning since I stayed up until 4 a.m. watching late movies. I really conked out after that.

Talked to Martha, Joan (her ceiling fell down again) and Rick who has spent the whole weekend counseling his twenty-four year old niece who has family problems. Rick has such a good heart and is always there with a clean handkerchief, a smile, a hearty laugh, a listening ear and comforting sentiment. He says he's too old to stay up until three in the morning.

My mother brings presents yesterday – a bracelet that my father brought back from Bermuda for me many long years ago, a lovely blue dressing gown with a white satin collar, a beige lambswool vest, a pair of pearly earrings and a hand-made blanket fashioned by my mother when I was a baby. Such treasures. My parents have given me so much. I begin to get a sense of my history, that I have been, and still am, the loved child. My feelings of abandonment are equally valid as are my memories of feeling loved.

What contradictions we all are. I suspect that part of the growing up process is to learn how to integrate those two opposing forces of love and abandonment – that something else is necessary to bring about the balance – a third force, perhaps detachment from both feelings. Perhaps it is called forgiveness. All children probably have similar feelings. Not all of them manage to grow up unscathed.

I now have two African violets. The first one was given to me by Mother O., as she is commonly called. She has been twenty years on dialysis. The other one my mother brought yesterday. Finally met the young woman, Sharon, who has been so good to my parents. Just knowing that they have someone to call on in case of need has relieved my mind about the situation. I feel sorry that I cannot offer my parents more support in their advancing years. Sharon has helped to fill in the gap.

Restlessness arises again. I want to scream at those walls, the closed door, the shuttered window. There is nothing that interests me although I have plenty of projects to work on. I watch TV listlessly. I doze. I wait for Richard to bring me my nightly coffee and cookies. My bum is sore from all the shots of Demerol, Gravol, antibiotics. My stump hurts. I savagely chew gum as if to take a bite out of all the things that bother me, to smooth out my aggressions.

My restlessness has to do with the fact that I feel I do not write well. I think I know what I want to say and how I want it to sound but then I discover that it doesn't measure up to my expectations. I am disappointed that my expectations, my imaginings and dreams have not come true. How I am and how I think are worlds apart. I am annoyed at myself when I cannot express myself, when I cannot write.

I am angry at the way my parents treat each other. I know it is none of my business, but it hurts me to see them undermine each other's confidence just when they need confidence the most. I know they are both most unhappy with themselves and each other. They are unable to change what I consider to be an intolerable situation. It disturbs me so much I can hardly stand it. Sometimes I get caught in the middle and feel like they are two dogs fighting over a bone – and I am the bone. They fight for my attention like two vaudeville entertainers. They fight for my love, my approval, my confirmation, my acknowledgement that they exist. I'm tired of all that – and it makes me restless. Maybe they are my petty tyrants.

I fall into the same trap every time to complete the conspiracy. My strategy has always been to ignore it – or get sick. Now it is time for some new tactics. What about laughter as a possibility?

Richard and I talk to Grandma. I really love that lady. She is such a wonderful spirit. She has not been well all summer – one thing after another – so we commiserate about our respective ailments. She sounds bright and cheerful tonight, and she always likes to hear from us. We try to call every few weeks or so. It does us all good. Dad Brennan is in hospital for knee surgery on Tuesday and not looking forward to it. It will take a while before he is on his feet again. Seems we all are having leg problems – Dad's knee, my father's hip, my amputation. What next?

My father gives words of encouragement to Richard and his music. He says it is the first time he has felt Richard with that quality that comes from the inner voice. I tell him that quality has always been there inside; now he is projecting it outward. "Let your light shine before men" (Bible). Playing in the Metro all summer has made a big difference. It's taught him to be more aggressive, less self-conscious, more present to himself. He reaches out more to the passersby and just loves to entertain. Every day he has stories to tell of life in the Metro – some amusing, some sad.

I sit up late (4:30 a.m.) and sip water to cool my throat. It is very cold outside. I wonder how my garden is. I haven't seen it since June. I imagine it is a mass of flowers and overgrown with weeds. Next year I'm going to try the square foot gardening method. I have a book which gives lots of hints to make things easy for me.

I am drowsy now and think I could sleep. I ask for Demerol and feel the full effects of it. Wonderful pain killer but it makes me drowsy and I don't like feeling so drowsy, particularly when there is so much to do. Writing has become a bit of an obsession lately and I feel uncomfortable with myself if I do not do some every day. Like an athlete in training, I practice every day.

> *"What can I do?"*
> *"Become what you have always been."*
> (Carl Jung)

September 17

Sunny day greets me. The light is so bright I can't see a thing, but better to be blinded by light and warmth than hidden away in the shadows.

I am too harsh with my parents. I know that a large part of their anxiety has to do with worrying about me and I am unkind to them when their intentions are the noblest. It must be excruciating for them and they take out their anger and feelings of powerlessness on each other. I must try to be more tolerant.

Just sitting here at 7:30 p.m. waiting for Richard. It is dark outside and getting colder – foreshadows of winter. Dr. B., my surgeon, looked at my stump today and was surprised and delighted that it is doing so well. He wants an opinion from the plastic surgeon about a skin graft over the wound. Jokingly I asked if I'd be out of here by Christmas. He took it seriously and said, "We'll see." I was stunned. Will it really take that long?

September 19

Did absolutely nothing yesterday. Spent Monday night with my head over the garbage pail and wanted to make sure that the vomiting cycle wouldn't start again, so I dozed and dreamt and slept and stared at the wall. Feel fine today. My moods fluctuate whimsically. I seem to have renewed energy this morning, so perhaps yesterday was a psychic rest, a replenishing ritual.

Betty sends a tape – her friend Rana's response to my journal along with her own comments. It does me so much good to be with her. She has this marvelous capacity to make whoever she is with feel important because she listens. Listening of itself is not that unusual but it is the way she listens with interest, compassion and concern. She reinforces my good feelings about myself and my life – a confidence builder. And now she has given me great encouragement, incentive for continuing with the journal. I have written sixty-four pages in seventeen days – an average of four pages a day. Not bad for a lazy person.

Am anxious to start on my three-dimensional sculpture for Paul's show at the end of January. I have several ideas but need materials and space before I start.

Just caught the end of a Lilias Yoga program which I watch periodically, and it dawned on me that I could do some of the Asana (yoga positions) sitting in bed. I do the ones I can manage, then do modifications of the rest. Yoga will help to strengthen my unused muscles as well as help me relax. I hate doing exercises but if I can do them with Lilias on TV it is quite enjoyable. It is another "solution" to the boredom and monotony I frequently experience in hospital. The program is on every afternoon at 3:30 – a good pre-dinner warm-up.

It has taken me a long time to adjust to the space that I do have and the limitations my body imposes on me. Most problems are solvable if I can learn to live with my limitations. And it is always necessary to find some enjoyment in the solutions, not just drudgery.

Sesame Street is also one of my favourite programs. It's delightful – great fun. I am learning my ABC's and how to count to 12 and all about Big Bird and The Cookie Monster and the Snuffle-upagus.

My world expands once more. Just when I think there is nowhere to go, no further signs along this road, something happens and shakes me loose from the iron grip of hopelessness. I receive letters from Chloe, Betty's friend in Pennsylvania, who tells me a little about herself and her life. She had a whole leg amputation five years ago and is as active now as ever. Letter from Matthew who is depressed and discouraged. I will call him later in New York. Also a tape from Betty and Rana in response to my journal. People I know, people I hardly know at all come to my rescue. That has happened to me so many times in my life that I know I must have a guardian angel who works through all these marvelous people who just appear when I need help.

Matthew sends *Don Juan* on tape which helps get me through dialysis, and I have been negligent in not telling him how much his time and effort mean to me – and how I treasure his reading and the music he so carefully selects for each tape. What a friend he is and how lazy I have become.

Jean-Claude calls and will come to visit tomorrow. He is back at school, going through the shock of readjustment. Wish I were taking courses. I had to cancel my two classes and opt for a three-credit course which doesn't start until January. Surely by then I should be on my feet or be able to manage on crutches.

Listening to Rana's response to my journal is overwhelming. I am stunned that it could have affected her so deeply, and flattered that it could be useful for other people.

*In times of fragmentation, emergency and
stress, get your priorities straight, then worry
about the details.
First, fly the plane. And then,*

1. *Communicate*
2. *Confess (state situation clearly)*
3. *Conform (take advice from others)*
4. *Climb (get above the clouds).*

(Jim Kirchner)

September 20

I talked to Matthew for almost an hour. We talk of relationships,
love and all of the experiences of our lives that lead beyond the
experience itself and teach us something about ourselves. We have
always been connected through our solitudes which meet and
greet each other and most of all stay a respectful distance. No
interference here – readiness to help and support when needed
but no unnecessary interference. We have known each other for
twenty years and rarely in that time have we been in the same city.
We lived together for a few months in '68 – or rather shared an
apartment – but mostly it has been a long-distance relationship
through letters, phone calls, and now tapes. My absent friend who
means so much to me – especially in these last few difficult years.

Just had a bath and washed my hair. Every little thing I do is an
effort, but it is getting easier to maneuver – with a little help from
my friends.

I am shamed by Rana who is almost blind and swims ten miles
in one shot. I used to swim a third of a mile and thought I was
doing well. Now I couldn't swim one lap without exhaustion. I
admire that kind of tenacity. She is also a middle eastern dancer
and is in charge of a support group for blind people. She speaks
honestly on the tape to me. I am very touched by her lucidity and
enthusiasm. She is forty years old and full of energy – full of a full
life. Great capacity for living.

I like my new network of friends that I have met through Betty
– Chloe, Rana, Metta, Joan (sculptor who has family here in
Montreal). Betty has been so important in my life and now she has
opened up a whole new area for me. I feel frustrated that my Sony
tape recorder is on the fritz and is being repaired. So much I want
to say to Betty, to Rana, to Matthew. Eventually I will keep a tape

recorder with me all the time so that I can record my thoughts and feelings as they happen. Rana says that one of the good things about my journal is its immediacy: the honesty of the moment, no sugar coating.

Sometimes when I listen to the journal I feel that I am merely being self-indulgent but no one else seems to have picked up on that. How critical we all are of ourselves, how uncompromising in our personal assessment. It is interesting to see myself from another's perspective.

It is quite warm again today. Summer returns briefly. Dr. B. thinks it is time to move forward, cut off a couple inches of bone and close the wound, at least partially. I immediately felt sick when he mentioned surgery even though I want to have the wound closed so that the next phase of healing can happen.

Wonderful thunderstorm and pelting rain at my window. It calms me as always.

Had a visit from Jean-Claude – then later from Martha and my old friend Debbie S. They both lead very busy lives and I appreciate the time they take to come and see me.

Martha says it's time I got out of this bed. She's right, of course. If I expect to walk out of here one of these days, I'd better start with a few leg exercises at least. Sometimes I need a good solid kick in the keister. This bed is getting too comfortable in some ways. I'm getting so used to being here I am afraid to go home. Here everything is looked after – my meals are cooked for me, my bed is made, my floor is swept, the dishes carried away, the table dusted – all things I will have to do for myself at home. It's been over three months since I have walked. Right, Martha. Time to make a super effort and I'm scared. I'm also apprehensive of surgery next week. No matter how many times I go through it, I'm still nervous.

Simple pleasures are the most treasured.
(K.T.B.)

September 21

Trying to follow my good intentions, my resolution to get out of this bed. I have a walker and "hallway privileges" which means I can go anywhere at all in the hospital on wheels. I hopped around my room a little this afternoon, pruning my plants and tidying up. Felt wonderful to be "mobile."

My spirits lift from early morning blues to late afternoon optimism. I spend an hour being tested for nerve function – unpleasant minute shocks that tell the technician how well my nervous system and nerve endings are responding. Somewhat worse than the last time I had this test. At the end he stuck a needle in the muscle of my hand and I fell apart – painful beyond belief. I cried for five minutes – but at least I got back to my room in time for my yoga program. I felt so good afterwards. It's been a real up and down day. My moods are as unsteady as my leg. Both will get stronger as I make my "super efforts."

Lucy, my Spanish nurse says, "You want to know Lucy? I have two priorities – respect for the human being and respect for suffering. You learn through suffering. One day you will be a sage." I have suffered much. I have learned much. I am nowhere near to being a sage, though I sometimes talk as if I were one. How presumptuous.

I fear that the writing is diluted, watered down. Perhaps because I write every day, I do not feel the intensity of the highs and lows. That does not come through in the journal. At least I don't think it does. It is hard for me to tell since I rarely reread what I have written.

Chloe says the only thing she worries about is getting too fat for her prosthesis. I laugh, as it is also one of my concerns – a ridiculous thing to worry about, but very real. It's always the little things that plague us and bring us to our knees, like the thorn in the lion's paw or the slightly uneven pavement that causes us to fall. The big things are somehow easier to deal with.

Humour is a polite form of despair.
(J. P. Lefevre)

September 23

Crossroads: I finally finished the quilt, a project begun 4 years ago. The cycle is complete. Time for new adventures. Where will I turn next? Which road to choose?

Not much to say these days – I feel dried up, full of dreams and unspoken wishes. The restlessness of autumn, the memories of other winters as I work on my photo album.

The Queen arrives tomorrow. Snow in Alberta and Saskatchewan already – hardly seems possible. Rick and I read the

New York Sunday Times – read from the Book Section and Arts and Leisure Section about lives of the literary and artistic giants. Details of my very ordinary life. Somehow it all fits together.

The annual Terry Fox ten kilometer run to raise funds for cancer research. People young and old run, walk and push baby strollers, determined to finish the course with dignity and remembrance for an extraordinary, ordinary young man who had a dream and the courage to make it come true. We all have dreams, some more noble than others, each one just as precious as the next. Not all of us have the courage and determination to realize them.

Richard brings me coffee, Rick brings me cake. Betty calls to say she will come tomorrow, perhaps with Jim, perhaps alone. She says she dug up a spruce tree for me so that I would have something from the woods since I can't get there myself. I look forward to her visit.

So many wondrous marvels to discover, to nourish, to soothe.

> *There is no trick, no magic to life.*
> *If you want to do something, you just go out and do it.*
> (Terry Fox)

September 24

David M. called this morning. He and Rita are expecting a baby at the end of October. His new play is also being produced at the end of October. Productive, those two. We talk. He is afraid of "isolation" so has not been to visit me. He says, "Do you ever get a day pass, like they do at Archambault Prison?" I love the way his mind works, the connections he sees. He keeps Richard and me amused.

Betty brought tapes of one of my journals and a joke tape, a good luck "warm fuzzy" from Rana, a spruce tree from the woods and a bunch of dried ferns and grasses that have an Adirondack fragrance and remind me of some of the plants I used to use on Salt Spring Island to dye wool. The smell brings back so many pleasant memories, particularly since I have been working on my photo album all morning and looking at pictures from Salt Spring. Felt pangs of nostalgia and a question mark. Why didn't our lives work out in such a paradise? I forget how impossible it was to live with G., even in paradise.

Betty gives me energy – and a good back rub and foot massage. Jim talks about his summer in the north with his plane that he bought after obtaining a pilot's license. What an enterprising young man. His life seems full of exciting possibilities – a job in Austria, perhaps, a temporary position in Washington with the World Bank, a conference in Vienna next week, and many mountains to climb. His Christmas letter last year about climbing Kilimanjaro was inspiring and got me through a rather black period – just to know that there are still people out there making conquests and living out their fantasies. I think it's wonderful to cultivate one's dreams, to plant a beanstalk and slay the giant, to come out of the nursery and create one's own rhymes and stories. There is something wonderful and magical about such creation. Jim, the dream-doer, go for it.

Paul M. (twenty-five) drops in after being at the dentist. He talks about the movie *Quest for Fire* and the search for warmth and security. He tells me about rising early in the morning as a child at his grandmother's home and helping her to build the fire and sitting there in their pajamas and slippers with hot buttered toast and sweet cocoa listening to a familiar tale told by his grandmother, waiting until the rest of the kitchen was warmed by the fire in the kitchen stove. What a marvelous picture he painted of warmth and security, the familiarity of fire and favourite stories – the oral tradition that is passed on like an intimate treasure, a legacy of familial ties and undeniable truths. I can see the family, the tribe sitting in the circle around the fire – the protective, invisible, unbroken chain of generations keeping back the unknown powers of darkness beyond the ring of fire.

I have been a part of that circle, a part of the warmth and security. I have also been cast into the darkness to fend for myself. I have felt fear and longing. I have danced on the tightrope that is loosely strung between pain and remembrance. I have leapt from the ground for a moment and hovered like a moth above the flame before plunging wholeheartedly, foolishly into the centre of the fire. I have been consumed only to be integrated again, reunited, reinvented, refueled, recreated like the phoenix that is reforged in the furnaces of heat and light. I am part of the circle and partake of its central fire.

Paul and I talk of fear and silence, that there is no sound that frightens more than silence – and yet within its parameters is liberation. A woman enters an empty house late at night and is absorbed by the echo of her own footsteps. She opens her mouth to scream and no sound emerges. Paul is full of curiosity and wonder. That is his most appealing characteristic.

Supposed to have surgery on Wednesday – a revision of my stump. Shorten the bone, close up the wound. I wish the doctors would let me know what they are up to – and when. It is very frustrating and annoying – these demi-gods who forget that we are all very human and in need of reassurance. I may appear to have it all under control, but really I am a wreck. I throw up after lunch and am calm by evening. Richard has flu and is miserable.

2:30 a.m. and I am still awake. I slept earlier in the evening as is my usual habit and now I am wide awake. Paul and I talked about dreams earlier in the day and concluded that they are often prophetic and therapeutic. My dreams lately have been of a violent, frustrated nature – lots of negative energy that has no outlet in ordinary life. Debbie talks about "small dreams" in which she remembers certain smells that in turn spark off a series of remembered images particularly of a summer place they had up north. Strange that she should mention smells and their power to remind us of times past as I have been experiencing that very thing all day. We talk for over an hour and finally ring off after several "messages" to do so from the switchboard here – a series of impatient clicks of the phone that seemed to indicate the operator's annoyance that we were tying up the line so long. They did the same thing the other night when Matthew and I talked for forty-five minutes.

Tina Turner looking like the wild woman from Borneo. Dyed hair askew like an explosion in a spaghetti factory.

The writing has taken on more density but lacks the intensity of the earlier work. I feel a little flat at the moment but can't seem to stop writing, hoping that it will liven me up.

I like the quietness of the night, the silence that surrounds and comforts me, that is soothing and cool. It calms me as long as I feel safe. And I feel the presence of some benevolent spirit who gives me energy and strength. Almost as if I were being taught by some higher being, taught how to be patient and persistent in my vision of good things to come, a belief and reliance on the faithful, purposeful unfolding of my life, to trust in the path that leads through the darkness. I am not very good in the light as it often is too intense and blinds me. There is enough light in darkness for me to see clearly where I must place my next step. I look inward for this light and there is always just enough to illuminate my path and keep me from straying too far into the deep forest.

5:15 a.m. There is nothing on TV at this hour. I have always wondered why not. It seems to me to be prime time. It is so silent that I can hear my ears ring. Must be nature's way of over-compensating for the silence.

In the Baptist church, people are totally submerged to be baptized. Sounds divine. I wonder if they perform the ceremony at 5:30, at dawn. There is so much I do not know about other people's beliefs. I respect anyone who holds firmly to his belief.

The land is so full of silence, there is no room for sound.
(National Geographic, about West Texas)

September 26

9 p.m. Out of surgery, I hope for the last time. Felt a little sick to my stomach afterwards, but otherwise no ill effects. I seemed to come out of the anaesthetic rather easily. My eyes are not so good – fuzzy as ever – and I have the hiccups. Nothing too serious.

Midnight. Awake as usual after surgery. I am shot full of Demerol for the pain in my leg. It gives me almost instant relief for a couple of hours – then the pain starts again, on its relentless mind and body drain. I try to write when I am alert.

I drink cup after cup of ice water. First I shiver, then I am too hot. Always my body demanding attention, always wanting something, never satisfied. Mostly right now I crave ice water; my throat burns and is sore from the tube they put down into my lungs during surgery to help me breathe properly. I have an I. V. still running in my arm so I should be well filled with fluid by dialysis tomorrow morning. They will take the bandages off on Friday to see what kind of a job they did.

The electrician has installed a new light over the bed and an additional gooseneck lamp so that I can direct the light on my work. I need intense focused light these days to see what I am writing. There are always alternatives if you know where to look for them and who to ask.

I have been so angry the last couple of days, mostly because I was in the dark about the operation and didn't know what exactly the surgeon was going to do. Which in turn made me very irritable. That and having to wait for over an hour for a porter to bring me back from dialysis to my room. I was so pissed off last Tuesday that I wheeled myself back in a fury. Hard on the arms and only works if my blood pressure is high enough so that I don't pass out. It's certainly much faster than waiting around downstairs for nothing.

4:30 a.m. Pain, pain and another shot of Demerol that blissfully takes the pain away. Musical tone poems on TV. Sailing to the Yucatan – and this is November. Electrified bass, a little reggae and black people searching for the thunder and lightning. We all search for something to believe in. And when we find it, we make it our God, our salvation, our delight, our treasure to be shared at whim. "Cry Me a River" rends the cool night air – the lost souls in unison at 4 a.m. How many are sleepless like me?

The writing is more loosely spaced tonight – not so cramped as it has been lately. That must say something about my moods in general. Not so compulsive and frantic. Feels good to relax a little. I am glad the surgery is over – it should be the last for a while. Dad Brennan had knee surgery a week ago and is up already on crutches. Haven't spoken to him but Mother B. says he is getting along just fine, other than the frustration of not sleeping well and having his leg in a cast. He has had a bad knee for years and decided to do something about it now that he has more time. Sure hope it makes him feel better.

Sweet card from Mary Jane in Brockville. It is very touching to be still receiving cards. Now we're on the second time around. My wall looks rather full – certainly colourful.

I seem to be writing a lot about nothing. Perhaps because I don't have a whole lot to say and risk repeating myself over and over. After all, each one of us has only one story to tell and despite the variations it is still basically the same old familiar tale.

My father used to tell me the story of Kathy and Chaffey's locks (near Kingston). I requested the same story every night and it always ended by my father saying, "And do you know who that little girl was?" I would always answer excitedly, "Taffy Taylor" and we would both laugh heartily. I loved that story. It was very comforting and secure – and I was wrapped in the certainty of my father's familiar voice. Wonderful, treasured memory.

September 27

I wake to the sound of a gum-cracking nurse who wants to take my blood. She is fast and efficient and snaps her jaw full of gum in a

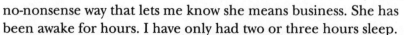

no-nonsense way that lets me know she means business. She has been awake for hours. I have only had two or three hours sleep.

Sun pours in although it is chilly. I wear my sweater over one shoulder due to I. V. in the other arm. I feel good considering it's the day after surgery. I look forward to breakfast. Throat still terribly sore. And my leg hurts. Complain, complain.

The feedback I have received about the journal has been overwhelming. Much more than I expected and I begin to dream. I like to think that I am not so much being flattered about these journals but rather being encouraged to continue. Richard is going to take the tapes of the journal to his father this week. I am so surprised that Richard has taken such an interest in my work. He played part of it for Bill, who also had good things to say. I wonder if it is because all who have read or listened are relatives and close friends. I still struggle with the price I will have to pay if the journal is ever published – the lack of privacy, the lack of control as to who reads it. So far my writing has been jealously guarded and to "go public" is a big step.

Back to the old dialysis routine. Again it took the porter almost an hour to come to the unit to wheel me back to my room. As a result, I almost missed my yoga program today and that puts me off because I rely on it for my daily exercise. The backlash from surgery still hasn't hit me.

Rick, then Susan, then Richard visited after supper. Rick read an article about Bette Davis which we all enjoyed. Susan brought roses and I gave her the scarf that I crocheted from wool she had given to me. Richard read a long letter from Aunt Mary and one from Edythe. Mary rambles on about a production of *Merchant of Venice* in her usual entertaining fashion. I love her letters.

2:30 a.m. Pain in my stump again. I call the nurse Marie for Demerol. She has a migraine and is most uncomfortable.

This Demerol is really knocking me out. I start to fall asleep but then I also want to write so I struggle against it and it takes a supreme effort of concentration not to slip out, to slip away into unconsciousness. The writing is terrible and I am scared that I will not be able to do it much longer. I feel a rising sense of urgency and frustration again that I may not be able to finish what I have started. The agony I feel is unmistakable and excruciating. Why do I allow myself to experience such doubt and lack of confidence?

Carnation

Richard and I talk about the early years when I first started dialysis – painful memories for both of us. We were both in shock and wondering how on earth we would be able to deal with the situation. It took a great deal of time and giving and learning. Now we are very close together. I rely on Richard though not in a cloying fashion which only suffocates and destroys. I want us to be close and I want us to be independent of each other. I need my solitude as he also needs his. We seem to have worked it out. We reinforce each other without false sentiment. It is wonderful to have a mate who is also my best friend.

Sure — tell me more. But tell me later.
(Richard)

September 28

Another brilliant fall day. The electrician is installing a new lighting fixture next door and it feels like the drill is going through my brain. Today they take down the dressing to see how the surgery went. Can hardly wait to see what they did and if it is healing properly.

Having a hard time staying awake today – dozed all morning. It must be my usual "delayed reaction" to surgery. Feel slightly low and not particularly motivated to do anything. Something is bothering me and I can't quite figure out what it is – and THAT bothers me even more. Sometimes a small change in the routine can make all the difference. I seem to need constant change and usually after some tension-producing event such as surgery I feel let down. It is as if I gather all my energy to deal with the immediate crisis, then let it all go – and let myself go with it. Psychic rest, Martha calls it.

3:15 a.m. Worked on my scrapbook for an hour or so but otherwise have done nothing all day. Even my yoga didn't help to recharge the battery.

Richard is starting a journal – says I inspired him. He writes so much better than I do. His images are poetic, his sense of balance and equilibrium so much more intact. I love to hear him read what he has written and hope he continues. He wants to encourage his father to record his life, his memories, his adventures. His father is such a good storyteller it would indeed be wonderful if he would put some of it on tape or write it down.

In my discontent, I eat a whole package of garden cremes. What is it that is nagging me? I watch an old movie on TV. It calms me. My stump is bothering me – and something else bothers me that is more difficult to identify. Ibsen's *The Doll House* is on. I have seen it before. I have the feeling these days that I have seen it all before. A profound sense of boredom sets in. Very little interests me. I am afraid to leave the hospital and all the responsibility that entails and yet I look forward to being able to walk again. Richard encourages me and I feel better, more confident. It is the unknown that disturbs me, that causes me uneasiness.

"Children of Gratitude": a phrase that speaks to me and puts me in my place. I have my life and I am discontent. How ungrateful, how disgraceful. It will all change tomorrow. That is the charm of life – that nothing stays the same for very long, that one can count on changes despite the seeming sameness day after day. I look for the affirmation of life and find my life wanting. I want to be quiet inside but am full of chatter and cannot seem to find my centre. I am on my edges and flounder at the end of an unbaited hook. It is the end of September and winter is almost upon us. I am missing the autumn, my favourite season.

Having trouble following a single thought because I cannot read what I have written and have to rely on memory. It is stretching my brain – good, but requires a new concentration. It is so easy to be discouraged by a stray thought or an idea. My mind wants to follow a new path to relieve the monotony, which does often make for difficult reading. My writing is small and cramped like my mind.

5:30 a.m. I seem to find relief and solace in the early morning. It is the beginning of a new day and with it new hope. I talk to Richard this evening about being facetious, saying that he must be honestly so. He starts to get at something, starts to reveal a little of himself, then gets nervous and lapses into silliness as if he were afraid or uncomfortable with the depths of his spirit. Soar, my love, soar; do not deny the river that runs deep within. Let it flow freely. You are clear as crystal, strong like the mountain, broad as the plains and you can fly to the highest point. You are the eagle; I am the dove with dreams of unbridled flight, free of gravity and the weighty tombstones we carry chained around our neck. When the burden is too heavy we lie down and bury ourselves in the soft, welcome earth.

What is this vacuum I cannot fill? I get peanut butter and melba toast but it does not satisfy my craving for an unruffled spirit. I look in all the wrong places for the right answers and find myself lacking, in want, desirous of a moment's peace. Sometimes I fly too high, move through the moments so quickly that I miss them entirely, lost in flight in a thunderstorm with no strings to attach me to the earth. I listen to rock 'n' roll and dance sitting down, waiting for the early morning news.

September 29

Huckleberry Finn at 6 a.m. He and Tom Sawyer and Robin Hood were my favourite childhood friends, along with Nancy Drew, the super-detective. I have always liked mystery – and nothing is quite so mysterious as the process of life itself.

Dreamt that my father and I were arguing and for the first time we managed to straighten it out. Progress.

You can't roller skate in a buffalo herd.
(From a Roger Miller song)

October 7

Could I begin to write again after a week's absence? I bottomed out for a few days, have spent hours lying in bed staring at the ceiling, waiting for the acute phase of depression to pass. I am still not through it. It overtakes me at the oddest times – just when everything seems to be going well. I finally forced myself to have a bath and wash my hair this morning and have not slept all day. It is a struggle not to give up.

I receive supportive calls from Betty and Richard's parents and a visit from my parents bearing gifts and encouragement. Richard rubs my back. Rick reads the *New York Times.* There is a merry clown from Sharon and wind chimes from Richard to ward off the bad spirits – yet I am weak and dispirited. Even staying awake is an effort. I want to sleep it all off like a bad hangover. This is not the way I want to live.

I write to try to expand my universe, to savour the all too-precious moments, the too-infrequent moments of aliveness. Writing seems to enhance my limited experience, make it more than it is.

Thanksgiving. Grey day; looks like rain. There has been a full moon so the tensions ought to ease up shortly. I hope this oppression lifts soon. I am worn out. I am taking steps to come out of my low cycle. When in trouble, communicate. I have called Martha, Joan and Debbie and have talked my way out of lethargy. Mother spent most of dialysis with me today and I feel so much better. She is so gentle and kind and just what I need to soothe my ragged edges. Perhaps I will be able to write again.

1:30 a.m. Wide awake, unable to relax enough to sleep. I turn on the TV to dull my mind or at least entertain me. Rick and Paul came over tonight and we had a slide show of Paul's pictures. I had a hard time seeing them but enjoyed the ones I could see. I think they were disappointed that I couldn't see more. I guess I was, too. People try so hard to please me and I can't always measure up to their expectations. I let it go and do not berate myself for my limitations. Their hearts are in the right place.

I try to start my exercises again to get stronger so that I will not be too weak when it comes time to start with the prosthesis. My physical confidence has diminished somewhat which leads me toward depression and discouragement.

I am being pushed down disturbingly silent corridors that disappear into bands of light, that break into disturbing patterns of shadow and doubt. I long for certitude and some relief from this shaky ground. At least my compulsion to write is intact. It feels good to want to do something active instead of sitting passively while my life passes me by.

My week of illness, self-indulgence, self-pity and self-absorption is past. A new cycle begins. Debbie and Ted visit for an hour or so and Debbie says, "Don't get too depressed or we will come to see you and try to cheer you up!" God forbid. We are good friends. It seems to me I have only had good friends since I learned to reach out for help in the last few years. Before that I was always too independent, didn't need anyone. How foolish I was and how much I missed.

I am fortunate to have such good friends and kind folk around me to help me over the rough spots. There have been many ragged times, many kindnesses. I feel such an overwhelming rush of new life – life that has been given to me, shared, freely flowing.

7 a.m. Awake to a cold, cloudy day. It is early and I am hungry and thirsty. My foot is cramped, my leg is stiff and in spasm, but I feel optimistic. What has changed and why is it now easier to deal with my life? It is all beyond me. There is something else operating here that has nothing to do with my effort, something that is whimsical and plays with my spirit. It is a devilish sprite, an elf that acts like a trickster and has its way at my expense. Today this little imp is gentle and treats me humanely, humourously.

Graham says I have one unfailing resource – my irrepressible ability to conceptualize, to get my priorities straight. He gives me hope and confidence that I can come through this latest depression, that I will find a way to overcome the uncertainty and self-doubt. I will lean on my own resources again.

I took a ride in the wheelchair this afternoon all on my own. Went to the sixth floor coffee shop and had a coffee and a date square. Then I found a ray of sunshine to sit in for a few minutes. It felt wonderful just to be on my own and out of my room for an hour. Then I did my yoga with the TV and felt even better. Now I just want to feel good. it is such a treat to feel pleasure in my body instead of pain. Lilias (yoga teacher) says to make an affirmation frequently throughout the day that we are the masters of our body, our mind, our emotions. The key is affirmation, saying yes to life in all its forms.

Called Paul to wish him happy birthday. We talked about sculpture ideas and materials, ideas, transformations, cycles. Lots of energy flowing between us. I got very enthused about doing some clay work. Paul will bring me some this week so I can give a form to some of my ideas.

Paul really understands what it is like to have been in isolation for such a long time. He intuits the necessity for outside energy that people bring in to me. He knows that I have very little energy to give back, that I rely on others right now to give me energy.

I am not writing well these days. I do not feel lucid at all – rather dull and anything but mercurial. I wish I could write well, brilliantly. I am such a dreamer.

Joan came for a visit after supper. I haven't seen her since August. Time passes slowly and we, the travelers, drift with it. I drift and sift the moments of my strange life. I am poured from the moulded pitcher that has been cracked and broken and mended so

often. My life oozes out of the fragments of crockery. I am fired at low heat, salt glazed, spitting explosions of smoky glass, tinted with amber and turquoise. No jewel, I, but imitation gem and stone.

5:30 a.m. How many nights have I wakened in pain, with this outrage which keeps me from sleep. It seems like a familiar habit. It is almost a familiar comfort to have my shot of Demerol to calm the storms inside. I wonder if I am addicted. It has been so long since I have been without pain. Am I addicted to the Demerol or to the pain? I drink cold milk to quench the fire which burns in my chest, to quell this savage beast which demands attention, which demands its due. All is silence around me. It is the darkest hour of the morning. I mourn for the light. Where is that ray of sunshine that earlier warmed my back, that comforted my spirit, that allowed its radiance to glance my way?

Yet I like the darkness hours, I like being penned here in darkness, in the unknown. Who knows what possibilities surround and enclose my prison? I can dream of ribbons of untravelled highway, infinite stretches of undisturbed beach, the rolling sea that washes up treasures from the deeper regions of Neptune's kingdom. I walk serenely on two whole legs. I am not blind. I escape from my physical limitations in another, more watery realm. If it weren't for gravity and the confines of earth I should be free in the elements of water, air, fire – and not be aware of my infirmity. Early morning flight through azure sky and sea, the purification of fire and water. Could I be transformed to some great sea bird, some mercurial phoenix that transcends time and space and soars aloft with gentle wing?

I face the unknown alone and I like it that way. This is my life and I can do with it as I will. My gift is darkness and the solitude it brings. It is 6 a.m., the cherished hour for reflection. Other voices awake, each wrapped in a little darkness, each ready for another day of light or whatever the coming light brings.

I cast my line into foreign waters and always find the relic of an abandoned treasure ship. What marvels lie at the bottom of the sea? Will I recognize them again today? Or leave them intact for other voyagers, other adventurers?

What we, who pass so swiftly, experience as songs of love or cries of pain are only overtones to a single note in a very much larger harmony.
(Lyall Watson)

I will probably be going to a rehabilitation hospital in the next couple of weeks. Will be glad to get out of here, at least into a different routine. This routine is boring me.

All my realizations are so common, so insignificant. I'm working for something that will change my life, my perspective. I feel so small and petty; I want to grow tall and strong like a great tree in the forest, like a great wise man. I want so much. I am too full of need, too full of myself. I need to be emptied so that I may be full again. I feel so restless, discontent. I think only of my pain.

Karen, my favourite nurse, lost her baby. I feel so sorry for her. It was her first and much longed for. She is having a hard time accepting it. She had a 36-hour labour only to deliver a dead child. I can't conceive of the grief she must feel. I don't think I could handle it.

Called Debbie and Martha to try to break this depression cycle. When in trouble, communicate, then confess and climb – à la Jim K., aeronautics engineer. It works almost every time. At least it's better than crashing all the time.

Sweet Richard brings me a mass of maple leaves – red and gold and amber. He scatters them all over the window ledge and tapes them to the wall. He brings me coffee and gum and tries to relieve my "cabin fever."

2:30 a.m. Wake as usual in pain and call for Demerol. It only helps for a brief while, then the pain is back along the suture line. Idiotic Elvis movie again. There must be something better to do with my time at this hour of the morning.

I may have to ask Graham for an anti-depressant. I feel these ups and downs too acutely and I am tired of being jostled around so much, not knowing from one minute to the next where I am at. Feel tossed like an empty bottle bobbing on the sea, taking in water that will ultimately drown me.

I'm sure I am addicted to Demerol. I wait for every four hour shot like an addict, nervous and sweating until relief comes. I like the momentary high. It doesn't last long enough to keep my spirits up and that is what I want. Confessions in the early morning.

The autumn slips away. I am missing another season. I feel the loss of familiar fall smells and sights. I have always loved the periods of transition. My body feels it is missing some sort of essential transformation that I need to go through for my sanity. Mental stability for me depends on emotional transformation. When I am static, I tend to feel bizarre, erratic. I need fuel, stimulation, change to burn.

October 11

Our language changes with our experience. I think of the space shuttle and the term "deep space." That phrase is so expressive – deep space. If only we could reach that level within ourselves and explore its dimensions, collect data, experiment with what it feels like to live there.

Richard took me to the early bird special run by the hospital ladies' auxiliary – a pre-Christmas bazaar with baked goodies, decorations, collectibles, hand knits, knick-knacks, etc. We bought some Christmas cards and looked around. Then I had coffee and muffin in the coffee shop. Went out in the chair again after supper, this time with Susan as my "pusher." We talked for two hours. It is so good to get out of my room. I do it at every opportunity, but still I am restless.

Marie gives me a shot of Valium to relax my muscle spasms. It seems I live on drugs of one kind or another. Anything to calm down. No wonder I'm so crazy. Even the Demerol seems to have little effect now. I worry about addiction and I can understand how one becomes addicted. There comes a time when I just don't want to deal with my life on any level, when I crave oblivion, when I reach for crutches and the easy way out. I am tired of the daily struggle to pretend that everything is okay – the face I show to the world. The plain truth is very opposite and I want to keep it to myself.

I am afraid of being cut off if I move to another hospital. An adventure surely, but again I plunge into the open sea wondering if I will survive or sink to the bottom like a stone. They will find me years hence all covered with barnacles and seaweed, a corpse for infinite probing and study. It all seems so senseless, the cycle of life with no transformation for me in sight.

Depression, elation, balance. I harbour them all. More Demerol. I think at last I can sleep.

October 14

Home for the afternoon. We drove along the lakeshore to Ste. Anne's. Fall colours everywhere. Uplifting to be part of the seasons again. Restless and depressed when we got back to the house so asked Richard to being me back to hospital. It is so awkward at home with the wheelchair. I have such a limited space to move around in. Do hope the prosthesis works.

October 16

The gloom lifts for a short while. There is no particular reason for me to be depressed. Everything is going well. Richard and I have a heart-to-heart last night – one of the few. He talks to my deeper self, sees beneath the surface of my complaints and recognizes that human condition in which all of us are occasionally trapped. He understands the laws of gravity and inertia that I have to struggle against, that we all have to struggle with. I feel I am wrestling with angels who are only trying to help me with no intention of doing me harm. It is, as Richard says, necessary to do something simple – merely a movement of the hand or legs can overcome those laws and can start the energy moving in a different direction, toward something positive.

He tells me a story about a "bag lady" with her shopping cart of worldly goods whom he saw one morning near the Metro about 5 a.m. She walked over to a park bench and began doing push-ups against the bench. He realized it was her way of working against gravity and inertia – that it was her way of staying alive. The story haunts me. And I want to get moving again.

4 a.m. Wakeful night. Can't seem to relax or fall asleep. Jean Claude came by about 8:30 in a student panic about the future. I told him what Richard told me, what Graham told me today. Focus on something simple in the present and the future will take care of itself.

So simple to see other people's problems,
so difficult to see one's own.
(K.T.B.)

October 18

Interesting how it is possible for me to see the confusion of another and help to sort it out when I am so empty myself. This has happened twice in the last couple of days. Maybe it is *because* I am so empty myself that I am better able to listen to others and be used as a sounding board for them to straighten out their tangled thoughts. I offer few suggestions but perhaps it is my presence itself that helps – and the fact that I listen to *them* rather than responding on the basis of some theory or other. Theories only serve to restrict. I have to approach people with a willingness to be raw, naked, vulnerable. In this state of vulnerability it is possible for real communication to take place. I treasure those moments but cannot hold on to them, for when I try to recapture that moment, that state, it eludes me and is lost to my awareness.

Trying to set the wheels in motion to get out of isolation. The time has come to be in more vital communication with my surroundings. I wheel myself up to the 18th floor sun room as often as I can and look out over the city. I meditate sometimes. Today I knocked over a glass table and broke it – then asked the head nurse if I could come back to her floor; my timing is not great. She said she would go to bat for me anytime – as soon as there is a room available, it'll be mine. Isolation is not a good place for me to be right now.

I get around in the wheelchair fairly well and when I get stuck there is always someone there to help me out. It is my imagination that gets in the way, telling me that I'll never make it through this or that door, or what if I get stuck on the elevator and on and on. When I actually go out there, I find it is much easier than my mind tells me it is.

There are some things that the mind does not do very well – like imagining what the future, or even the present, will bring. It is just that – imagination that so often has so little to do with reality. Reality, the moment, is so much simpler. If we could only learn to live in the present instead of being two steps ahead.

Richard reads to me from Krishnamurti's *Think on These Things* about discontent that is based on wanting more but a kind of discontent that is a quieting of the mind so that the creative can be released. I am not sure that I understand exactly what he means by discontent or joy although it seems to have something to do with inner growth, inner peace and self-awareness.

Long letter from Mary which Richard reads to me. She writes "newsy" letters which I treasure – about what she thinks and feels, about daily events and family – always amusing and in such a way that I can hear her voice talking. I keep them all in a file marked "Letters from Aunt Mary."

Mother sends me three very elegant bed jackets. They are all silky and make me feel like a grand lady. She also brought a shawl that she made when I was a baby. Then it was a blanket; now I use it as a shawl. Another precious treasure from my precious mother.

October 19

It is midnight and I have moved upstairs to the 18th floor for a little while until I am transferred to a convalescent hospital. Already I feel my spirits lift as I gaze out the window overlooking the city. The lights burn on into the night. There are others who travel through the darkness, shedding light on the path. I do not feel alone, accompanied as I am by these pilgrims of the night.

I am so much affected by my surroundings. Here there is space, air, open doors – and I feel unbounded. No more isolation. It is quiet even though the doors are all open. I can hear the laboured, regular breathing of the patient across the hall. The sound is somehow comforting, as is the ticking of my clock. Reassuring in a night so dark. I listen for signs of life. I listen and am still, following my breath – inhalation and exhalation – the regularity comforts and reassures me that here is a life and here am I, awake amidst a sleeping world.

4 a.m. Wake up uneasy and in pain. Can't seem to sleep the night through without waking at least once. I wake on the edge of a dream about Betty and old friends. We climb a mountain together. We see much unusual, exotic foliage and plant growth. The names of the plants are familiar as they grow rampantly through the hillside. The pathway is steep and I have climbed it before. We keep stopping to have lengthy philosophical conversations. Eventually we reach the top of a craggy cliff and all of us are very quiet as we listen to the waterfall crashing fall below. There is no thought of going back down. I am comfortable here.

My eyes are doing strange things these days. When I close them, my mind immediately forms a mental picture of what I have been looking at. I must have thousands of such pictures stored in my brain.

October 20

Just rereading some of the letters I have received while in hospital. News of old friends that I grew up with. They all seem to be building cottages or redecorating their homes. I think about all my childhood friends and realize how strangely different my life is. It seems somehow that my life *ought* to be more like theirs, more settled, more stable – but it isn't. I was always too restless and discontent, too eager to find alternatives to the lifestyles in which I was brought up. Now I live in an immigrant area, collect a disability pension. Most of my friends are ten years younger and single. I wonder if I would have been happier if I had never left Brockville.

Lately I have felt a strange longing to move somewhere else. I do not want to go back to Coloniale Street. It no longer feels like my home. I want a different sort of life. I'm tired of living like a Bohemian. I want space and air and light. I want to be able to stretch out my arms and breathe deeply of the richness of the world. Unbind my wounds and float like a butterfly.

I wonder sometimes if any of these drugs really get to the source of my pain. I wonder how real my pain is and if I would be better off without the drugs. The pain is real enough, but what causes me to feel it the way I do? I am a slave to my pain and I am humble before it.

I am also enslaved by my lack of strength. I marvel at the physical capacity of others and the apparent ease with which they move about. They do not seem to be aware of that privilege that allows them to undertake and complete even the simplest of tasks – to walk, to bend, to reach, to stand firm. I am astonished that any of this is possible at all.

The sounds of late evening are becoming more familiar. I can hear at least two people breathing as they sleep. The signs of life around me; ever changing, ever the same. Breathing in and out. In and out. So calmly reassuring. When the nurses do their rounds at night to check on the patients, they stand quietly in the doorway and listen for the regular breathing that signifies all is well. As long as there is breath, life goes on.

Suffering is not an illness: it is the normal counterpole to happiness. A complex becomes pathological only when we think we have not got it.
(Carl Jung)

October 21

Sunday at Brooks' in the country – rain all day. Talked and played *Trivial Pursuit*. Restless. Depressed. It is the Demerol? Can't write. Want relief from this life of pain and struggle. Tired of it all.

2 a.m. I hate to admit it but I feel better after finally getting a

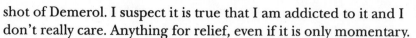

shot of Demerol. I suspect it is true that I am addicted to it and I don't really care. Anything for relief, even if it is only momentary.

The day in the country was quite lovely. It hurts me every time I go out to realize how helpless I am and it bothers me that Richard has to carry me into the house as the terrain is too rough for the wheelchair. I hate being such a burden to him and hope that it doesn't last much longer. This weekend pass is almost more than we can handle, although it does me so much good to have a change of scene. Now I feel relaxed, no longer suicidal as I did earlier.

It takes so little to push me over the edge. Mostly I am optimistic with brief interludes of despair. I am too sensitive and easily hurt. The trees are bare. The leaves have fallen. Winter is not far away. I do not look forward to it.

I hate the hassle with the wheel chair every time we go out. Richard has been so good to me. I expect one of these times he will explode with rage and both of us will feel awful. I don't know how he copes with it in his own mind and heart. I had a good cry before he left tonight. It is so damned difficult, not only to keep my own spirits up but to be as little trouble to others as I can. I am fortunate that the people around me have been very patient and kind and willing to help. It could easily be the other way; I shudder to think about it. It's been enough having to be carried over the rough spots, but to be a burden, a restriction on other people's lives is hard to take. I don't mind my own limitations but to place those restrictions on others is darned difficult. One of these days Richard is going to rebel.

I dread the coming of winter and its confinement. No use worrying about it now. I must take it in small steps. Nevertheless the future seems threatening and gloomy. I am afraid I will end up in a wheelchair and I desperately do not want that.

6 a.m. Thinking about the day, and realize that I am afraid I will not be able to handle other people's reactions to my "handicap." I know what it feels like from the inside to have severe limitations, to be dependent on the kindness of others. I wonder how others feel – if they are ill at ease or if they take me for granted. I notice that even old friends treat me differently, more cautiously. And strangers eye me with curiosity, say nothing and then often ignore me. I think I would prefer people to be startled into asking a question or two and then treat me as they would treat anyone else.

Today was fine but I felt uncomfortable, as if I should explain why I couldn't move from my chair. How self-centered I have become, always worrying what other people will think, make jokes about. I am always concerned about being pitied or laughed at. My ego is my worst enemy as I struggle with self-importance.

It's better to burn out than it is to rust.
(Neil Young, from "Hey, Hey, My, My")

October 22

I seem to be losing my self-confidence. I feel fine in hospital where everything is done for me – meals cooked, bed made, help getting to the bathroom, medication for sleep, for pain, etc. I dread going back to the apartment which is so small and impossible in the wheelchair. I can't even get into the other rooms. I *must* learn to walk.

Yesterday Richard said he was glad he didn't have to carry me around all the time – that, and the awkwardness of the wheelchair is difficult for him. I am surprised he hasn't blown his stack yet. He has been so patient with all this. I worry that he will get so fed up he will leave me, although in reality I don't think he ever would. He is too loyal. Nevertheless, it is constantly on my mind these days.

Perhaps it would be a good idea to talk to him about my fear. He says so little about how he feels and is such a stoic. Like a mountain. Or rather, like a volcano that could explode at any time without warning. I feel the suppressed rage in him and it frightens me, disturbs me – as I don't think I will be able to deal with it. I live under a cloud of uncertainty and self-doubt. I wonder what happened to the girl who was manager of a book store, who completed a communications diploma, who made films, who used to swim three times a week, who walked six or seven miles a day ...

Dr. B. says that the worst is over. I feel that the worst is just beginning. I do not feel courageous or even particularly motivated, I'm full of conflicting emotions and can't seem to get my priorities straight. Got to get back to day-by-day existence.

Richard reassures me as we talk about my fears. We hold each other and I feel safe once again. How little it takes, how easily I fall apart, how easily I mend.

Shake me I rattle,
Squeeze me I cry.
I am reminded of this song. I only remember these two lines. I think the next two are
Please take me home
And love me.
Strange the things we remember.

October 23

It is almost too bright for me to see anything at all this morning. All I see out the window is white light. No sign of the cityscape at all. I feel as if I were in another galaxy except for the room I have become so familiar with. I remember the fantasies of childhood and the wonder I felt at everything around me. I also have always had a very private magical world in which I was in control of every event which took place. Of course, I was always the central character in the dramas that I invented. Sometimes I wish that this latest development in my life was just another fantasy that I could re-create, change, forget whenever I get tired of it. Not so. This is a reality I cannot change except by adopting a new attitude. It is so difficult to break old habits. I do not want to let go of the old patterns. I am in transition between the known and the unknown. Perhaps it is always thus.

I just used the walker for the first time in two months and did quite well with it. Immediately my confidence level rose about 100%. I actually walked out into the hall and back. It feels fantastic to be standing up.

Dr. B. has stopped the Demerol. If I am addicted, the next few days may be difficult. I do not look forward to it. Uncertainty. I will also soon be transferred to a convalescent hospital for rehabilitation. More uncertainty. Breakfast, physiotherapy, dialysis, lunch, nap, coffee shop, supper, visitors (usually only Richard) TV, sleep – same routine, same faces, same me. On and on.

I am acutely restless tonight. Can hardly sit still to write. My legs keep cramping and I am in pain. Finally I get a shot of Demerol. Abrupt withdrawal is too hard to take. They will have to do it more gradually, gently so that my body has a chance to adjust. I went through several hours of hell and brimstone. Now I feel calmer, more coherent. Demerol is one of those drugs which relieves pain almost immediately. Perhaps that is why I became addicted. So pleasant and soothing to my frazzled nerves. It allows me several moments of peace and release from torment. But then I want that all the time, so I get addicted to it.

Sometimes I don't care if I am hooked on it. I know intellectually with my mind that it is no good and eventually leads to depression when the effects of the drug wear thin. But the relief outweighs any ill effects. I feel lighter in spirit and calm in mind – free of pain both physical and emotional.

I have an addictive personality – tobacco, booze, dope – all of which I have given up. Now I am addicted to food and eat and drink (water, coffee) far more than I need. There is an emptiness buried deep inside that I cannot fill. I try to fill it with all the false idols and temptations of our planet. None of them fills up the empty spaces. So I turn to meditation and the teachings of Gurdjieff to guide me through this maze called life. My emptiness helps me toward spiritual growth, but does very little to help me in my day-to-day existence. The restlessness and boredom are my constant companions. They accompany me everywhere, riding on my shoulders like demanding children who insist on attracting all my attention. I need to be clever, to give them their due – at the same time doing so on my own terms and not being suffocated by them. At times I feel their grip around my neck.

To learn to wear restlessness and boredom like jewels, with grace and dignity, would be an accomplishment. I strive for that. I strive to fill my time with useful work – although I am not very good at it yet. I can only try to do so momentarily. Most of the time just passes and I am passive, carried along with its whims. At other times I create my life; I actually participate and direct the scenario. Only then do I feel alive – when I can perform the simplest task because I wish to do so. It is called going against the laws of gravity and inertia. Very difficult, because most of the time, I want to be lazy and just lie around and let someone else make the effort.

I find it more difficult to be interested in anything these days. Perhaps it is because of my eyesight. Perhaps it is just the general nature of my life. I admire people who approach life with enthusiasm and curiosity. Once I was eager to try new things; now I am more hesitant. The eagerness will return. I am sure it is a matter of time. In the meantime, I spend many hours waiting for who knows what.

We are all passengers on life's journey. Just passing through.
(K.T.B.)

October 24

Having a hard time without the Demerol. I am restless and depressed. I can't seem to find anything that interests me. I stare at TV or off into space or doze.

Just watching a program on self-healing. The dialectic between the explanation and the mystery. What kind of people are we that we could heal ourselves? We have the ability to do so. But to tap that source, that powerhouse.... I know it is possible. Many have done it. Why not me?

2 a.m. Sleepless night as I eat peanut butter and crackers. I turn on the TV to some idiotic program, take a Valium to relax and drink cold coffee. I like the night time with its comforting darkness that surrounds and protects me. I try to hold on but feel my life slipping away. I fill the emptiness with food and water. I cannot take hold of anything. Everyone tries so hard to encourage me and I take their efforts and swallow them – no response.

October 25

Sunrise over the city – a rare treat. Rose and yellow wash over black buildings. A haze of hues.

October 26

Trying to turn my life around. After one of the worst days I've had in a long time, I decided to make a few changes – like getting dressed every day and continuing a crocheting project started months ago. I am already doing healing exercises twice a day and physiotherapy for my legs and general strength. I need to be hopeful again. I need to feel the possibilities as realities. I need to fulfill some dreams. And I will.

It is important to realize that each day brings me a little closer to the day I will walk out of here. Important to realize that each day is important and not just to be tolerated, suffered through. Each day *means* something, *is* life and ought to be lived with respect.

Joanne and Paula (dialysis nurses) took me to the hospital Hallowe'en party at midnight. Two hours later I finally came back to my room. I had a great time – even danced in my wheelchair and talked to a few people. About half were in costume – gorilla,

Arabian prince, the Pope and many more. People do love to wear masks.

*The only masks we cannot remove
are the ones that we wear all the time.*
(K.T.B.)

October 27

Finally found my legible pen again. Interesting how that coincides with my change of spirit that is now clearer, lighter, more lucid – not thick and heavy as it has been these last few weeks. I talk with Tom D. who advises me on the conservation of energy – not to go the limit and burn out but to save a little, like a yogurt culture to be used to make more. I tend to burn out and then have to start from zero. We talk about tension and allowing it to be released.

I sit in my wheelchair in the sun room overlooking the city lights and the night sky after a long day at home with Richard. It is the first time in four months that I wanted to stay home. I wanted to be well but was content to sit at our kitchen table polishing the silver in the fading light while Richard read to me from his journal and sang his music. I felt once again that I was home at last.

Everyone keeps saying that the worst is over. Perhaps they are right and all my needless fears of the future are illusion. Perhaps that future that I fear so much does not exist; perhaps I am only a dreamer who will awake to a different reality than the nightmare I have imagined. Images, images. Mirrors of sadness, reflections of gloom, untrue, unwilling to recede, haunting me with their reality. Who is this dreamer? What power dares this dream to have over a helpless dreamer who cannot act in any real sense. I am the dreamer and the dream and only I can awake myself from the slumber of a soundless sleep that threatens to hypnotize, mesmerize, etherize the dreamer which is who I am.

I sit and stare at the cool evening-scape of city lights, remembering the warm orange of the lamp on our kitchen table at dusk. I am content to have lived this day. All there is is life, and life is all I have, to give my heart away in the flush glow of living it. I do not want to sleep anymore. I want to be awake and aware.

3 a.m. So glad to have my pen again. It makes all the difference to my thinking. Clarity reigns for the moment and I see more clear-

ly where I am going, where I am. Most of all I feel at peace with the raging demons. My sleep is unhaunted by nightmares. The phantoms have gone to sleep for awhile, leaving me to dream in silence without jeopardizing the dreamer.

Why experience so much in order to forget it afterwards?
(P.D. Ouspensky)

October 29

I scream this afternoon at the top of my lungs. It's bad enough that I have to learn to walk again, I don't need problems with my fistula, too. Give me a break. Shit. Piss. Fuck. I'm fed up with all this goddamned nonsense. It's enough already. Half the staff came running. By the time I had reached the end of my expletives I was laughing. I'm such a bad patient, I said. Ann, Martha, and Paul laughed with me. I feel tremendously unburdened. Such an explosion, that sent shock waves through the unit. I don't even feel guilty about it – more relieved than anything else. I got rid of the frustration of these last days in a moment. So good to get it out. I hope it didn't disturb anyone else.

Richard takes me to see David's new play, a reading by the Playwrights' Workshop. I think he was quite pleased to hear his work which is offbeat and full of very personal clichés. He writes as if life were a cliché but one that hasn't been heard before. Some marvelous lines that originate from his wily sense of the ridiculous and his witty perceptions of our mass media, neon-plated, nickel jukebox world. Bill and Paul helped me and the wheelchair up and down stairs. Not too trying – with a little help from our friends. It sure does me worlds of good to do normal things. Nothing seems insurmountable with Richard, et al.

Yesterday a phone call from Betty that cheers me up immensely. We talk of our lives, our bad times and the good. Both of us had a tough week but are through it now. Another call from Joy in Brockville who has been flat on her back for two months again with a disc problem that may require surgery. We commiserate about isolation and immobility. Life is so easy for some people, but for us at times it is the pits and we always wonder why we have to go through these dreadfully difficult passages. What are we supposed to learn? – if, in fact, we are supposed to learn anything at all. The question remains a mystery.

My friend Joan takes me for a walk in the afternoon of a perfect fall day. We roar up and down the sidewalk, laugh, make comments on the passersby, have coffee and muffins. Later we prowl around the gift shop and she buys me a pair of smashing silver earrings which I really love. She is such an unusual friend – very bright, very funny, very witty.

It must be something cosmic, a law of gravity pressing down on our frail spirits – all one can do is wait for it to pass like a thunderstorm. The deck gets shuffled again, the roulette wheel spins for delight or grief. Place your bets, ladies and gentlemen. *Rien ne va plus.* You pays your money and you takes your chances. Win or lose, it's all in the game. Aces are high, jokers are wild and everything in between is anybody's guess.

5 a.m. Tylenol and cold, cold milk. Refreshing during a fitful sleep. Stump bothers me and keeps me awake. I will be so happy when they remove the stitches. They are made of wire and tend to dig into me.

Where is the bridge between happiness and despair? Why do some people leap from the bridge and others manage to make it to the other side? Could they exchange identities in the middle and be transformed by girders of steel, a firm structure that is meant to carry persons across to distant land or perhaps back home? How to build such a structure within that is firm and true and will not collapse in the wind, that sways ever so gently and crackles once in a while as the steel contracts and expands due to temperature changes. Moody are we who have waited so long at the foot of the bridge, waiting for the final gun to go off so that we may start our personal marathon. We look around at our neighbors and compare stances, compare determination, compare victory, compare defeat. Does it really matter what the other guy does? As long as we do the best we can.

November 1

Howling November wind that forebodes winter and perhaps worse. The sun shines on not-so-white buildings. They look so heavy from up here, as if they were about to crush the earth, to sink into the ground – or as if Mother Nature were about to heave one great sigh of relief to get them off her back, earthquake style. It is a time of great upheaval in many people's lives. I hear it all around me – perhaps it is always thus and we are more or less touched by it depending on the state we are in ourselves.

I think I am through my great depression for now. I keep busy with clay and wool and writing. It is difficult to find the self-motivating force, for I am indolent and sometimes self-pitying.

He whose face gives no light should never become a star.
(William Blake)

November 2

Writing has slowed down to a halt. I am questioning the worth of all these words and sentiments and of what possible value they could have to anyone other than those who know me well. I start with such a flourish, then something happens and I start to doubt, to flounder, to perish in my own enthusiasm. What is this cycle of disrepair that takes everything apart and is so difficult to put back in place? Disrepair is the right word – all the parts are there, it's just that they are not functioning together and have their own method of cohesion. It is I who cannot cope with the flux, the change that has taken place.

I am no longer "sick" and find it difficult to be well. I expect more of myself but still want to lie in bed and be waited on, ring the buzzer, call for a nurse when I know very well I could figure it out for myself and accomplish the task with wheelchair or walker. I want to be well and out of here, but sometimes the effort is too great. I resent having to make such efforts all of the time, yet feel so much better when I do. That old feeling of accomplishment and small success – the look of joy on a child's face as he ties his shoe for the first time.

Why don't I feel this joy when I walk a little farther each day? It is only afterward that I can allow myself to feel pleased – at the time, it is always as if I should have tried to go farther. It is very frustrating, this learning process.

Diane, my physiotherapist, has been wonderful. She keeps up the pace and encouragement and will not let me be lazy. I try a little harder when she is around.

I keep looking forward too quickly to the goal, the end that is so
dimly in the future, instead of taking it one step at a time.
I am bored and impatient with one step at a time.
I want to be able to run before I can barely walk.
(K.T.B.)

November 3

These last few years have taught me much. I used to be so frantic – what a waste of time and energy that was! I want to say that to so many people: "Slow down: danger zone." I wish I had learned that lesson early.

We have a busy day. Home for the weekend; wash dishes, bake a chocolate cake with raspberry cream cheese icing. Richard makes quiche and vegetables for supper, I write letters. Ted and Debbie drop by for cake and chatter, Paul with his mercurial mind that makes impossible leaps and risks. He loses his audience because he moves too fast but I love to try to follow. He is full of the wonder and intensity of being twenty-five.

Good to be home. I feel so normal and easy-going, loose and friendly towards all, including myself. My attention is drawn by many things. There is so much I want to do. This healing process is slowing me down. I have difficulty being patient and persevering.

I watch the idiot box and am annoyed at how noisy it is, how cacophonous, inharmonious, unpleasant, as it shrieks and screeches, slams its message of unconsciousness across the room, howls and furls its preconditioned, carefully prepared habit-forming advertisements into the peace between me and it.

I do not like the space around me to be too full. It chokes and suffocates me. There is such a thing as being smothered by impressions. I have been so isolated, confined to such a limited environment, that I am overwhelmed by the "real" world. I am protected from it to a large extent, or rather have been limited a lot lately. I have passed through a cycle, a stage, very quickly. None of this growing old gracefully, and though I have grown rapidly older I sometimes feel I have retained a certain grace – a freedom and acceptance that has allowed what is, to be, without too much complaint.

I have allowed for the anger, the fear, the joy – given all a space in my life – expressed it vociferously at times. Fed up, damning everything, every unfairness, just leave me alone, give me a break; if it isn't my eyes or my kidneys, now they have taken my leg and I have to suffer every time I see someone walk across the room. I am insanely jealous of runners and yet I marvel at the wonder of it, all in the same breath. I let it all out, the conflicts, the contradictions, the confusion, the quietude and eventually the calm.

I am angry, yes indeed, but at the situation rather than specific people. I have created my life and I will deal with it in my own way, on my own terms. All I ask is to be allowed to do so without too much interference. I want to be free to make my own choices, but most important, to have alternatives, a card or two up my sleeve to pull out in triumph when the circumstances of my life would have me believe that I am losing ground.

I write of things I do not know. I write of things I wish for, like a cosmic Christmas list, a grocery list of the galaxy. And yet I want nothing.

It is so quiet now. I hear the sink give its last gurgle of recognition, the 'fridge as the motor shuts off, the hot water heater as it finishes its cycle, my pen as it scratches, etches black markings, hieroglyphs of a modern era, across these smooth white pages. I hear Richard snort a couple of times as he tries to settle down between incalculably cold cotton sheets. I hear ringing in my ears that sounds like the seashore I remember – the ebb and flow, that sudden rush of water over pebbles and shells left behind on the beach. I cannot sleep. The sounds are still too loud. As it gets quieter around me, it gets noisier inside as my body must compensate for the silence. I am cramped sitting in this wheelchair, hunched over this book, catching the warm orange glow from a lamp I made many years ago.

I must concentrate on very small spaces in order to see; my range is narrow, my vision limited, my spirit clear and fresh in spite of all the set-backs. I go forward with fear and curiosity, with awe and trembling for the path that lies ahead of me. Would it were always thus.

There is something intimate about this orange light at our kitchen table, the scratching of the pen, the cold pre-winter night when my foot aches from lack of circulation. I feel secure, here in the darkness, without the bombardment of images, voices, slogans, metaphors. It is so simple just to sit and listen, to allow yourself to listen without compulsion, even without comprehension. It is unnecessary to understand everything.

There is a butterfly pinned to the wall above the table where I write.
Would that I could free that butterfly and allow it to fly
as it was meant to; would that I could free myself and fly too.
(K.T.B.)

132

Sunday morning activity. I make muffins. Richard makes coffee
and eggs. Rock and roll on the radio, warm smells from the oven,
sun streams through our kitchen window. I watch the last few
leaves refuse to give up their tenure to winter's approach. They
flutter stubbornly in the wind that tries so hard to dislodge them
and hurl them to the frozen earth. Yet the leaves persist and the
wind persists, knowing that it is just playing a part in nature's
relentless cycle. We too must persist as we play our various roles, as
we live our little lives, like leaves clinging to a sometimes sapless
tree, sometimes to a tree in full bloom or a tree at rest. We hold on
with such will, such tenacity, such tenderness. It is always awe-
inspiring, this firm, sometimes tenuous grip we have. It is as if trying circumstances only serve to strengthen our resolve to never let
go of that which is this precious life – and at the same time teaches
us that we must let go if the cycle is to continue.

Richard practices his singing – ma, me, mi, mo, mu, mo, mi,
me, ma. The birds chirp outside. I listen and am grateful. I can still
hear the wooden chimes that we hung from the tree last summer.
They rattle like dry bones as the wind brings them to life. Even the
dead are living today.

It is evening now and I am still here. I sit at the kitchen table
listening to Richard play the piano, sipping Kahlua. I do not want
to go back to the hospital, for this place is full of music and poetry
and peace. The winter winds have quieted now. I am still. All is stillness. No whining, whistling, whamming wind to disturb the simple
breathing out and breathing in. Richard sings his sorrow, his job,
his eternity, his mortality as he plays unfamiliar chords. When he
stops, that means it is time to go. I do not want him to stop. I wait
uncertainly for the signal that sends me back to a life of routine
and frustration, where I am a patient trying to be a person. What I
miss most in hospital is Richard's music, his spirit which seems to
glide on harmonies and even on discordant sound waves.

He pauses for a moment, a few eternities pass, he begins anew
the old lament, slower the pace, clearer the words and notes as he
experiments with sound and voice.

... I remember yesterday, we had no place to go ... minor key, a
dominant seventh here and there, a major triad, a single note as he
explores, expands, ranging further afield, now returning to the
familiar melody ... seems like yesterday, we went away before ... no

words yet.... Chords in the making. Magic. Mystery. I hear rain on the window pane, soft, gentle, healing; not lashing, searing ... how do you know that yesterday ... goodbye yesterday ... and are you happy so far away ... seems like yesterday ... seems that we threw it away ... and are you happy now?

November 6

I am deluged with "messages" these days – like the old man who came stumbling toward me waiting at the elevator in my wheel-chair, cane in hand. "Don't despair," he said, eyeing my sawn-off leg. "I have one of those, too, and I manage just fine."

Then our friend, poet Bill F., crawling over the mountain in a blinding rainstorm, soaked inside and out, having just had fight #39 with his current lady love. A taxi pulls over and the passenger, a black musician from Georgia, orders the cabbie to pick Bill up. He says, "There's hope a-comin,' brother."

And today as I sit quietly in the sunroom, a perfect stranger says to me abruptly, "Do you knit? I have some wool I'd just love to give you." I was about to refuse but reconsidered and said yes, how wonderful. People amaze me with their resilience and hope – who am I to refuse anyone's gift and the pleasure they have in giving it? I pass all this on to my friend Joy in Brockville who is still flat on her back with disc problems. Like a found penny that is only lucky if you pass it on.

The midnight hour has struck. Our friends David and Rita have just had a baby girl. And so the cycle continues – the cycle of birth and life and growth and dying and death. Somehow every-thing happens in proper order with an unmistakable rhythm and majesty. There is no point in doing battle with the seasons. They will always be. We must pass through and not interrupt their progress.

November 10

Back to the kitchen table, to 50's rock and roll, to blue jeans and homecoming queens, daydreams in Levi's – it's been that kind of day. Drizzle and grey and reflective surfaces, mirrors of memory, intimations and intonations, sound waves that echo through a darkened corridor. The lights went out in the hospital last night. I lay in the darkness, absorbing the silence, reflecting on my solitude as Florence Nightingales floated through the hallways with their incandescent lamps. "The sisters of mercy, they are not departed or gone" (Leonard Cohen). Their reassuring voices rose and fell, spreading confidence and encouraging confessions in the twilight.

To be uncertain is to be part of the river of life. To be otherwise secure is to stagnate. We spend so much time searching for certainty and stability. We forget that life is a transient experience that is always full of uncertainties and flux. We embalm ourselves, protect our fragility, entomb ourselves with solid and decaying barricades that only shut us away from the mystery, the ever-changing magic that is in us and around us. Dare to be uncertain, strive for fluidity, take the risk of losing it all. Live in the open, share the wonder of life in its inconsistency and mobility, its impermanence, its preciousness, its vulnerability.

Nancy and I talk the other morning in the sunroom. She is an amputee also, of Welsh extraction. She reads to me an article about ghost-hunting in Edinburgh. "Are you scared?" she asks. "Do you believe in all this? I do." She starts to tell of her experiences. She tells of her husband Stan, who died many years ago and who appeared to her one cold winter night to tell her there was something wrong with the furnace. She said that he was also present during her difficult surgery and helped her to recuperate. She told me that years ago, when her husband was rushed to emergency in the Toronto General Hospital, she had said to the doctors afterward that she believed a miracle had saved him. The doctor said to her. "You know, we never go into surgery without a prayer first. We need it more than you do." She is a very remarkable lady and determined to walk again.

Another remarkable person came to visit me while I was on dialysis the other day – Joan H., a friend of Betty's from State College who grew up in Montreal and was sent to Miss Edgar's and Miss Cramps' exclusive girls' school in Westmount. Joan is in Montreal for a few days to celebrate the 75th anniversary of the school. We talked as if we had known each other for years. She looks like Betty and I see why they are such close friends. It is interesting to meet people who are close to someone that I am close to.

I drift, I dream, and then I too must come back to zero. My energy is spent. I have given all to my dreams and there is little left over. After the dream, it is always back to basics. Richard writes about self-indulgence. I drink Kahlua and coffee. Self-indulgence. Self-discovery. It's all okay as long as I have a sense of humour, as long as it doesn't become self-pity, self-recrimination, self-justifica-tion. Self-indulgence – another trap to spring in the quantum leap through self-doubt to self-knowledge. But always with a sense of humour, a sense of blithe perspective.

Overtime. That's when the regularly scheduled game is pro-longed to give an opportunity to one side or the other to score the winning goal. It is an attempt to declare that some of us are win-ners and some losers and the water goes down the drain just the same. Does it matter who wins and who loses? The laws of gravity and inertia will never change.

Richard's friend Jacques says I am much calmer than I used to be. Sometimes I feel he is right. I feel more centered, less frantic and scattered. We sit here by candlelight at midnight listening to the radio and the ever-so-subtle raindrops on the window pane. It is all so integral to our lives – the light, the music, the patterns of rain, cloud, sun, shadow. We live as if tomorrow will always be there, knowing that it could disappear at any moment, that we could be left with no future, no hope, no dawn to wake us. And what if tomorrow comes? What will we do with it? Will it be the same as today? Or can be change that? Could we be different today so that tomorrow could be different as well?

Live each day as if it were your last,
because one of these days, you'll be right.
(Leo Buscaglia)

November 11

Sunday. Remembrance day. Richard has the music in him today – he plays guitar, piano, voice. I make muffins, crochet, write, make a tape for Betty. It's a rainy, cold Sunday afternoon in November. Soon it will pass away into memory, another link in the chain of life.

November 13

First snowfall blankets the city. I watch from my window as the buildings grow whiter and whiter. The usual strident, garish sounds of city life are muffled by the snow. Quietly, quietly, it falls.

December 11

New leg. I am a miracle of modern medical science. She talks, she cries, she laughs, she walks. After all these months I finally stand on my two feet.

December 18

Have been home since Saturday, December 15 – almost 6 months since I entered hospital on June 19. This house feels so familiar that I shed the last few months easily. I sit and read the newspaper (I can only manage the headlines), I polish the silver, I bake brownies, I scrub pots and pans until I am satisfied with their glow, I wrap presents, I write Christmas cards, I wash my hair and adore the sound of Richard's guitar. I am happy to be back, in my little nest. This last month has been particularly trying. I can't seem to remember exactly what it was that so upset me. All I know is that if I had not come home when I did, I might have been lost forever. I was getting so used to being waited on that I was becoming very lazy and could very easily have become more crippled than I am. It's not so bad operating from a wheelchair as I will be doing for a while before my stump toughens up enough for me to be able to wear my prosthesis full time. If I were confined to a wheelchair permanently it would be another story. As a temporary vehicle, it is very useful and always a challenge to invent new ways of doing all the things I am used to doing for myself.

Had a letter from Jim K. a few days ago which arrived when I was feeling very low and unsure of myself. I burst into tears as Ann read me Jim's ever-so-flattering words that spoke of the journal and the impact it had on him, his admiration of my courage and the way I had chosen to meet the challenges in my life. He, too, is a conqueror and has the adventurer's spirit.

I wanted to write some brilliant words after all this time not writing – this hiatus in hell – but whatever bitter taste remains has been sweetened by my return home and I have little to say about what has happened.

I watch the winter closely as it slips by with hardly a trace – no snow, yet the trees are bare, the ground cold, the birds fragile but singing with determined spirit. I have never watched so closely, finding in its passage a likeness to myself and my spirit. I find within myself a darkness that resonates and begins to vanish in ever decreasing echoes. As the last reverberation dies in me, I greet the morn with gladness that I have made it once more through the fire. I have choked on clouds of smoke and I am seared and burned by flame and I am weary of my losses and I have paid the price of knowledge and experience, I have paid with my blood and my breath. Yet I bleed, yet I breathe.

I think I needed those six months to adjust to the shock of losing a leg. It is like a period of mourning after the death of a loved one, the loss of a part of myself. There can be no real replacement of that. Things will never be the same again.

Yea, though I walk through the valley
of the shadow of death, I will fear no evil.
(Psalm 23)

December 24

The winter howls round the streets, the ice forms on the front steps. I sit alone by the heater warming my body and my heart. I feel misty and slightly sad that nothing will ever be the same again. I feel a sense of loss and now another impending loss as my stump has a small discoloured patch along the incision line. Also my middle finger of the left hand. When will this relentless process slow down? Must I spend the rest of my life waiting silently while this disease takes its toll and I die by pieces. It is a long way to journey's end.

We spend the afternoon around the kitchen table with Paul, who brings a record and Jean-Claude, who brings a spectacular cactus. We drink coffee, talk about Wim Wender's latest film, and music, always music.

January 4, 1985

I have been home for almost 3 weeks. I spend long hours sitting by the heater warming my feet and hands, trying to recapture a fleeting and elusive moment of peace. I am still in shock after the events of the last few months. I feel the loss even more acutely now that I am home. The surroundings are familiar yet there are corners and heights that are inaccessible. I find new ways to do the same old things yet I have little joy in the doing. There are few highs, only varying degrees of lows. There is little that interests me. I clean out drawers and cupboards hoping to find a fresh starting point, a place to begin again at this, the dawn of a new year. But I am violated and unable to forget the unfairness of it all, remember only what I have lost, not what I have left.

January 14

Middle finger, right hand is bothering me and has done so for two weeks. It keeps me awake at night – that and Richard's coughing. It is 4:30 a.m. I am back on codeine. It is cold at this hour of the morning as I write by the light of the kitchen lamp. Pitch black outside. Silent except for the ticking clock and the gas heater going on and off.

I brought my prosthesis home for the weekend and wore it twice on Saturday, twice on Sunday for an hour or so. I am slowly getting used to it.

January 15

At school tonight waiting for Richard to pick me up. I'm taking a course in the history of animated film, taught by our old friend Bob, who says in the first class last week that animation is the re-creation of movement (rather than the recording or photo-graphing of movement). Interesting that I should be taking this course now as I relearn how to walk, as I relearn how to recreate movement.

I pick up a schedule of films being shown at school and immediately feel greedy when I see what I am missing. I feel deprived, cheated and want do so much more than I am able to. I am desperate for stimulation, hungry as a young bird. I want so much and feel so limited in the choices that are open to me. Even to arrange to go to a movie is a major production. It used to be so simple. I am tired of "making do," tired of making the best of a rotten situation. I sit and watch out the window as life passes by in front of me and I feel very separated from the mainstream.

January 16

Walking well today – the prosthesis almost feels comfortable. Can it be that I am finally getting used to all this?

I look forward to the ice cold gingerale that Anita brings to me when I come to dialysis. It clears my head as well as soothes my throat. I get up at 6:30 on dialysis days so that I can get a ride to the hospital with Pat, a most congenial taxi driver who drives many of the dialysis patients back and forth to the unit. He even carries me to and from the cab at no extra charge. He used to be a bar-tender – also plays drums and says he is a "nasty son-of-a-bitch" when he gets mad.

It is 2 p.m. and I am finished with dialysis for the day. I am sitting here in the unit waiting for Pat to take me home. I have had yet another painful day and am speechless with torment and the absurdity of it all. I have been asked to fill out a questionnaire regarding whether or not I would want to have dialysis continued if I were to become so ill that I was confused during waking hours or unable to take full responsibility for my actions. I am being asked very politely if I would like to die. I find it all so ludicrous.

February 1

For the first time in days, I am free of pain. I sit here relishing the experience, imagining what I could accomplish if I were like this all the time.

February 3

I am out of the habit of writing and feel the threat of timidity as I try to compose my thoughts and reflections on this last dry period. Varying degrees of depression come and go – the cycle becomes much too familiar – at times it is almost a comfort, a safe place to retreat where I can justify my inactivity and inertia. I need no excuses – after all, I am almost blind, handicapped, etc., etc. I do not need to be courageous here, hiding under the covers; it is enough labour just to breathe. I do not even want to eat or drink – just lie here feeling that there is very little left for me – yes, I have many days like that. But then something stirs deep inside, something that wants to live and be vital and grow, something that is curious and longs to see what is beyond the boundaries of my prison, something that remembers the richness of past experiences, something that longs to connect with other life forms. I am like a heavy clod of earth by the riverbank that tires of watching the river flow by. I break away from the earthen mass and am swept up in swirling currents, dazzled and delighted by the movement around and through me. I let it carry me back to life, to be part of the river again, dangerous and delicious in the uncertainty of what happens next, knowing only that I will move in some direction of which I have as yet no knowledge.

February 5

I was dreaming about the end of the world and it was very funny and very sad and very truthful.

February 12

Waiting at school for Richard to pick me up. I am so desperate these days for outside stimulation. I see no one, I go nowhere except to the hospital for dialysis. I cannot read and my readers are all too busy with their own lives. I sleep more than I need to and am depressed a great deal of the time. I write little. The days are bitterly cold, the wind tears at my thin black coat, I bury my head in my hand-made scarf. My circulation is poor, my hands and foot suffer the sting of the cold. I worry that I will be further incapacitated. It is winter and I feel its severity, its rawness and indifference. It is dark when I rise at 6:30 to go to the hospital and it is a lonely and harsh cold that greets me as I leave my bed. I know there is an end to it. For the time being, I lie underground and try to protect and store my strength for the growing season to come.

My restless spirit emerges from its wintery cocoon occasionally and searches for ways to find flight, to soar unbounded. I feel the weight of the albatross round my neck like a fallen crown of thorns. The images are bloodied, torn from a heart that still beats and cries out for life. It has been so long that I have been encased in cold steel.

April 20

Now that I am beginning to adjust to being one-legged, my hands have started to give me trouble and cause me grief. They are so incredibly sensitive that I can hardly bear to pick up a pen and write – but I am compelled to record this passage through the darker regions. My days are full of anxiety, my nights are full of pain ...

> *I want only to touch people so that they remember*
> *that we are all here for such a short time*
> *and that we have much to learn from each other.*
> (K.T.B.)

Katharine Taylor Brennan died early on Sunday morning, April 21, 1985, at Montreal General Hospital after being a patient for only a few hours. Funeral services were held in Brockville on April 24, with interment in Oakland Cemetery, Brockville. A memorial service was held in Montreal on April 27.